TOURISM and
TERRORISM

TOURISM and TERRORISM

✦

An Experience of Turkey and the World

PROF DERMAN KÜÇÜKALTAN

iUniverse, Inc.

New York Lincoln Shanghai

TOURISM and TERRORISM
An Experience of Turkey and the World

iUniverse books may be ordered through booksellers or by contacting:

iUniverse
2021 Pine Lake Road, Suite 100
Lincoln, NE 68512
www.iuniverse.com
1-800-Authors (1-800-288-4677)

ISBN-13: 978-0-595-38998-8 (pbk)
ISBN-13: 978-0-595-83389-4 (ebk)
ISBN-10: 0-595-38998-8 (pbk)
ISBN-10: 0-595-83389-6 (ebk)

Printed in the United States of America

Contents

List of Illustrations

List of Tables

FOREWORD

When world events are analyzed, terrorism may be seen primarily as affecting tourism and tourists. In other words, the sectors that are targets of terrorism often are those that have thriving tourism. Indeed, the one thing that terrorism and tourism have in common is that both deal with human beings. While tourism is associated with peace and humanism, terrorism is associated with antihumanistic and blood-spilling acts.

For the last thirty years, and especially after the events of September 11, the opposite concepts of terrorism and tourism have moved to the global platform, each having an effect on the other. This type of interaction is not arbitrary. When the "global monster" known as terrorism is studied, it may be seen, unfortunately, that terrorism will continue to associate itself with tourism into the future.

The economic, political, and social chaos that is brought about by the partnership of terrorism and tourism reflects not only in a national context but an international context as well. This prolongs terrorist activities, while decreasing tourism.

This book discusses the reasons for and development of the connection between terrorism and tourism, citing examples in Turkey. The chapter titled "A Sample Model Oriented toward Terrorist Acts" was written thanks to the contributions of assistant professor Dr. Adil Oğuzhan, head of the department of Econometry at Trakya University; I am grateful to him. I also would like to thank Mehmet Yılmaz, lecturer at Gelibolu Piri Reis Vocational School in Çanakkale Onsekiz Mart University, for his assistance in the preparation of this book; Dilek Gökalp, Instructor Alper Aslan for their contributions; my wife, Gül, and my son, Berk, with whom I have shared the hardships and rewards of academic life, and iUniverse, who published the book.

I am responsible for any omissions or discrepancies that need correction in this book.

Turkey, January 2006

INTRODUCTION

Tourism has felt the repercussions of global crises due to the elasticity of the market. A crisis situation of national and international dimension affects tourism, perhaps more than any other sector. A nation's tourism brings value to its economy, and that value is seen in other sectors as well, either directly or indirectly. Thus, crises have negative consequences on a country's micro- and macroeconomic stability. Tourism today is called an "industry without a chimney"; that is, tourism dollars remain in and benefit the country. Tourism also potentially increases employment and gradually improves a country's economy. This important industry is directing countries' economies at the turn of the twenty-first century.

The "Global Tourism 2010" presentation from the World Trade Organization (WTO) projects that tourism will continue to steadily progress, with an expected 1.6 billion tourists internationally by 2020.

Such rapid development in tourism has many underlying reasons, one of which is a growing interest in formerly unfamiliar regions of the world, coupled with better transportation and more relaxed travel across countries' borders. This upsurge in tourism is evidenced by the fact that the number of international tourists grew from 550 million in 1994 to 760 million in late 2004. When the number of domestic tourists is added to this figure, it is easy to recognize the broad economic dimension of tourism.

As in any business, demand stimulates supply—there has been a rapid increase in accommodation and transportation facilities and in the infrastructure facilities in those countries that cater to tourism.

Countries develop various products for tourism, diversifying their products in order to increase their market share. For this to be effective, however, the economic, demographic, cultural, social, and technological changes in the world must be taken into account; thus; tourism becomes a dynamic structure.

For instance, political changes in the world have altered the profile of trade. Countries of the former Eastern bloc, especially, have revived a type of economic tourism called "shuttle trade", a travel that foreigners take a vocation for shopping.

An escalating adult population in European countries, where tourism is strong, and in other industrialized countries has brought an increase in "third age tourism" (a travel for people of 50 and over); this indicates that the third age group should be considered with regard to tourism supply. Just as importantly, youth tourism is an important source of demand in certain countries, including Turkey, and that creates economic productivity.

Interest in various world cultures has led to an increase in tourism in those countries that effectively market their cultural values. As a result, travel has improved to areas with a vast historical and religious past.

That is to say; while technological and social changes have led to positive progress in international travel, such changes often have had a negative effect on countries' natural resources. People tend to gravitate away from areas that have environmental pollution, heavy industrialization, noise and physical pollution, and destruction of flora and fauna, opting, instead, for natural areas where such unpleasantness does not exist; this has led to a demand for "rural tourism."

Such changing consumer preferences bring an increased demand for elasticity of tourism demand (sensitivity of tourism demand to cyclical fluctuation). Security also is an important factor that affects tourism demand. Global terrorism had affected tourism in those areas where terrorism is most likely to occur. Seasonality is an important factor in tourism as well, but the frequency of terrorist acts or terrorist threats have a strong impact on tourism businesses and tourists alike.

In the first chapter of this book, the concept and types of crises are covered. Among the types of crises, terrorism is given significant mention, along with its definition, extent, and types.

In the second chapter, the reasons why people travel are suggested, as well as the relationship of tourism and terrorism, Examples are given with regard to Turkey and the world. In this context, the events of September 11, which were the crescendo in the ascendancy of global terror, are analyzed.

A pilot model, conducted on a selection of tourists visiting Turkey, is offered as an analysis of studies on national crisis management and businesses facing terrorist events. The media's approach toward terrorist events, sine qua non for terror, is presented, with examples from Turkey and the world.

1

TERRORISM AS A TYPE OF CRISIS

1.1. The Concept and Scope of Crisis

Crisis may be defined as "distress, misery, depression." In a wider sense, crisis is "an uneasiness that exists in a turning point for better or worse" (Dinçer, 383).

A crisis in economics, for example, is "a periodic fact that reduces cause-and-effect-oriented consumption (demand) in agricultural, industrial and/or service sectors" (www.wikipedia.org/wiki/Crise).

With regard to medicine, crisis is "a sudden change in the course of a disease or the turning point of a disease for the worse when it is not healed" or "the certainty that recovery is no longer possible" (Tekelioğlu, 185). Particular fields of medicine, such as cardiology, psychiatry, or neurology, have more specific definitions of "crisis."

Crises may be classified as micro, macro, and global, according to their scale. Micro-crises involve one or a few businesses. Macro-crises can have repercussions on macroeconomic indicators, such as budget, export/import, current account balance, inflation, and GNP, when no precautions are taken. Global-scale crises rapidly can spread to every country in the world when economic borders are demolished. The interaction of these three crises can be seen through real examples in the world.

While it is possible to foresee some crises, others cannot be predicted. A crisis situation necessarily restricts the decision-making process, as it requires making calm, urgent, clear, and right-minded decisions in a limited amount of time. If rational decisions are not made, the prevailing crisis can result in new crises.

One effect of globalization is that it enables crises to spread rapidly, but it also helps certain countries think of new alternatives to dealing with crises. Globalization refers not only to the flow of technology, labor, and money but also to the disadvantages of that technology, labor, and money—a crisis can spread beyond geographical and economic borders. Tourism, due to its international dimensions, has become the leading sector affected by crises.

In a crisis environment, those who are on the verge of making a decision must be qualified to wait. That is why Herman defined crisis in business administration as "a situation that requires a fundamental decision-making process but gives no sufficient time, although it renders people responsible for decision making" (www.fr.wikipedia.org/wiki/Crise).

Many factors may cause a business crisis to emerge. These factors may be divided into two groups: intra-business and extra-business. Intra-business factors may include the deficiencies of CEOs, lack of experience and data gathering, business properties, and employee error during production. Although not particularly relevant to this subject matter, these factors cannot be ignored with regard to a quick recovery from crises.

The biggest difference between an intra-organizational (internal) crisis and an extra-organizational crisis (which happens outside an organization) is that the extra-organizational crisis can affect all the elements in an economy; that is, all sectors, even the global economy. An intra-organizational crisis, however, primarily affects a particular organization; a broader crisis may affect other organizations (macroeconomic politics) as well.

Based on these data, crisis may be defined as "a process in which an unusual, unexpected, or the least-expected situation occurs in a certain period." The duration and limits of a crisis can rise or fall due to the situation before and during the crisis, as well as the after-crisis performance of the CEO and his team.

A crisis period has numerous effects on the businesses of a particular country. Crisis properties are shown in Table 1. It is possible, however, to observe some of these properties in macroeconomic parameters.

Table 1: Main Characteristics of a Crisis Period [*]

CENTRALIZATION OF AUTHORITY	FEAR AND PANIC	DEFORMATION OF DECISION-MAKING PROCESS
—Supervision becomes centralized to a great extent. —Better supervision of activities occurs through standardization, intensification of supervision, or centralization of authority. —There is an attempt to remove internal liabilities caused by the environment, increasing the level of leadership, structure, and supervision. —The central decision-making unit is composed of homogeneous individuals who are united and directed by a strong leader. —The decision-making group becomes smaller. —A leader assumes authority or abdicates it, due to receiving threats. —Authority becomes centralized. —Autocratic behaviors increase during organizational dissolution and decision-making groups get smaller. —The impact of the crisis is centralized. —Authority figures take more responsibility for decision making.	—A regime of administrative personnel extends in a crisis period. —It becomes impossible to satisfy security needs, respect, and self-realization, due to stress. —A reluctant organizational climate is created. —Organization members withdraw; the amount of production decreases; irregular attendance and the period of operation (and thus, discontent) increase. —The crisis increases any precrisis struggles. —Administrators take care of losses, seek ways out of the dilemma, determine short-term solutions, take action with simple logic, and may panic. —Crisis threatens individual aims and creates inefficiency, disappointment, tension, and fear. —Physical and mental tiredness is often observed in individuals involved in crisis.	—Among the principal pathologies of a crisis are limitation of cognitive processes, deterioration of or deficiencies in the information needed for decisions, and lack of stability in programming. —Creative politics is essential but often is impossible to execute. —Paranoid reactions are characteristic of crisis behaviors. —Individuals exhibit a decreased ability to see all aspects of various situations due to stress. —When individuals are under stress, there is an increase in the number of mistakes they make, the process of solving problems gets tougher, the tolerance for uncertainty decreases, and the ability to look past complex problems lessens. The quality of decision making decreases. —Cognitive performance decreases as the level and duration of the crisis increase. —The organization dissolves during a crisis period and becomes unable to direct itself.

Table 1: Main Characteristics of a Crisis Period (Continued)[*]

CENTRALIZATION OF AUTHORITY	FEAR AND PANIC	DEFORMATION OF DECISION-MAKING PROCESS
		—The administrative decision-making process is more difficult, due to crisis management.

[*] **Resource:** Akat, İ.; Budak, G. et al. (2002): **İşletme Yönetimi**, İzmir, Başarı Yay, p. 412.

1.2. Main Types of Crises

Extra-organizational crises may be classified according to their sources and purposes. All types of crises, however, can influence each other. For this reason, a crisis environment in a region or country can trigger other crises on a national or international scale, much like the ripples made by throwing a stone into still water.

Although there are many types of crises, it is possible to identify the causes of all crises within the principal discourse of economics. Economics is based on scarce resources and infinite needs. This premise can help to identify the causes of any crisis because the same two principles are the basis of all types of crises: scarce resources and infinite needs.

When human beings' needs cannot be met by available resources, and when human beings have no executive skills, the situation naturally brings about crises. For this reason, the origin of all crises can most likely be found in economic problems.

Economic distortions and crises follow a cycle: economic problems cause a series of crises, and the existent crises form new economic crises. Thus, internal cycles trigger each other.

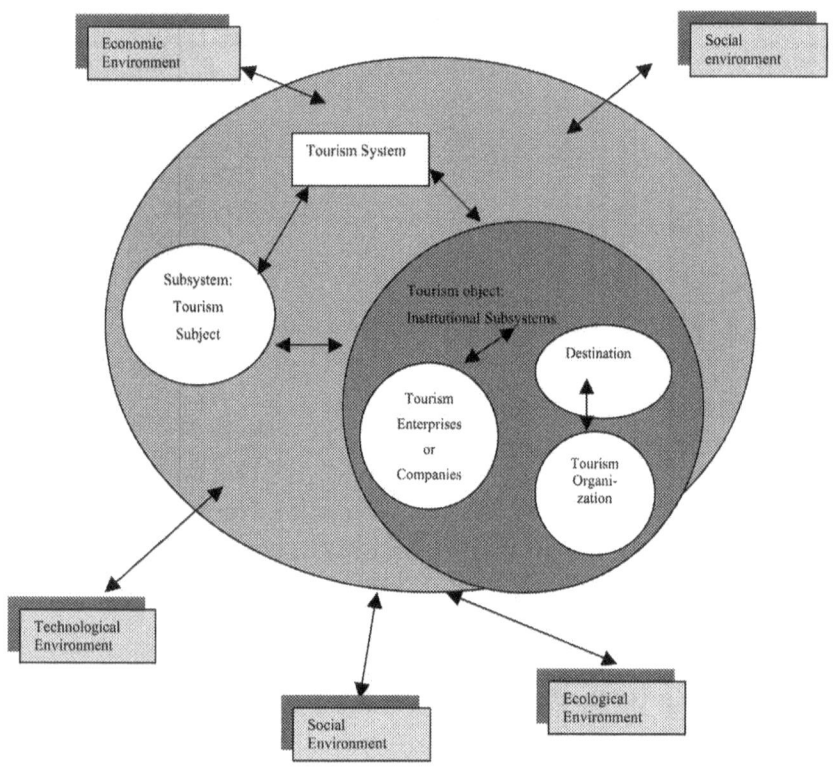

Figure 1: The Relation of Tourism System and Environment
Resource: D. Glaesser, *Turizm Sektöründe Kriz Yönetimi*, İstanbul, Set-Systems, p.16.

Figure 1 shows the various environments that interact within the tourism system. As shown, tourism interacts with economic, technological, political, and ecological environments. Crises that occur in any of the environments, therefore, easily can affect tourism.

Tourism ranks first among the sectors most affected by crises because the demand for tourism is sensitive not only to prices, income, fashion, habits, tastes, and preferences but also to conjectural fluctuations. Hence, tourism is greatly affected by extraordinary situations with periodic properties, such as crises. Crisis environments that occur in the tourism sector, where the multiplier effect is high, surely influence other sectors.

1.2.1. Economic Crises

Economic crises may be considered as cause and effect of other crisis types; that is, regardless of the type of crisis, it likely has an economic basis, and its effect influences economics.

Economic crises in a country may be defined as macro-economic shortages occurring in a certain period unexpectedly or because of inadequate or wrong administrative preferences. High inflation, devaluation, radical governmental monetary policies, and export shrinkage are among the main factors that cause economic crisis. Political preferences undoubtedly have a role in the emergence of economic crises, too.

Economic crises often focus on the financial sector and balance of payments. These crises can be the result of the financial preferences of the political authority in countries as well as in global markets, as economic decisions are, to a great extent, comparable to political choices.

Singapore, which is a major market, went through an economic crisis in 2002. Export to the United States dropped by 5.6 percent in the third quarter of that year, while other economies in the region (e.g., Indonesia, Malaysia, South Korea) faced economic recession.

Germany has been influenced by economic stagnation in Europe. The rate of unemployment in Germany in 2002 rose to 9.4 percent (www. ntvmsnbc.com/news/).

The economic crises in certain countries, including Turkey, affected not only the countries in question but also the global economy. The repercussions were advantageous for some countries, while other countries were placed at a disadvantage.

When an economic crisis is perceived as permanent, the dynamic structure of the global economy leads to new economic events, as do dense competition and rapid and effective restructuring of economic activities. Globalization, therefore, refers to the rapid spread of an event or activity from one part of the world to other parts of the world. For this reason, it is difficult to isolate a crisis to only one region or country.

World events that have taken place since the early twentieth century exemplify the reflections of globalization on world economies. The Great Depression of 1929 had a negative influence on the economy of many countries, including Turkey. For the first time in history, the Turkish lira lost its value and the prices of agricultural products, which were the most important export income during those years, dropped in international markets. Rising oil prices between 1973 and 1974 negatively influenced the Turkish economy, as was the case in other countries.

The oil crisis, which started with the invasion of Kuwait by Iraq in 1990, negatively influenced all tourism sectors in Turkey. The financial crisis in Turkey reached its peak with the United Nations intervention in Iraq.

After the devaluation of the Chinese yuan in 1994, Asian countries, such as South Korea, Thailand, and Taiwan, were impacted negatively because they produced goods similar to those produced in China. Additionally, Japan, a leading Asian country, could not move past its economic stagnation that began in the 1990s, which caused these countries to export fewer goods.

The economic and financial crisis that began in the Far East and spread to Russia and Brazil influenced the Turkish economy negatively as well. Shuttle trade receded from 3.7 million dollars to 2.3 million dollars in 1999, due to the crisis with respect to the previous year (www.dtm.gov.tr).

World economic crises create an immediate influence on international tourism demand. The rate of international tourists decreased by 4 percent in United States in 2002. The regression was 14 percent in South America, 34 percent in Uruguay and 21 percent in Brazil. (www.world-tourism.org/market_research/facts/highlights).

The economic crisis in Japan, a country that typically has 17 percent of the international-traveler traffic in Asian-Pacific countries, had a negative impact on the number of Japanese who traveled to other countries in the region, reflecting a 4 to 1.6 percent drop. The number of Japanese visitors subsequently decreased by 4 percent in Indonesia, 3 percent in the Republic of Korea, and 1.6 percent in Australia (www.world-tourism.org/market_research/facts/highlights).

Economic crises on a national scale sometimes reflect on international economic crises. For example, Turkey's high interest rates and internal borrowing in 1999 rose. An earthquake on August 17, 1999, caused an economic burden of such magnitude that a new economic program was suggested on December 21, 1999.

While the new economic program was viewed as a positive step, it caused a bottleneck in the banking sector in the last quarter of 2000, which resulted in government intervention for many banks. A financial crisis occurred after the intervention—interest rates rose, and the repo rate escalated by over 1000 percent overnight. When the Turkish Central Bank launched available reserve currency, aimed at stopping a possible rise in the foreign exchange rate, foreign exchange reserves decreased by seven billion dollars in three weeks, and Turkey lost its foreign capital.

This financial crisis, which began in the interbank markets on November 21, 2001, led to an economic depression three months later that was to become the largest depression ever recorded in the history of Turkish Republic. The resulting shock from the events of November 21st upset the markets and caused interest rates to reach an all-time high.

In the same year (2001), market speculations and a financial shock occurred with regard to Turkish lira, due to the reported tensions between President Ahmet Necdet Sezer and then-prime minister Bülent Ecevit. Funding to public banks was completely cut off, causing a bottleneck in public finance; the Turkish lira lost great value.

Subsequently, Turkish Republic Merkez Bankası arranged new monetary and exchange-rate policies. A floating exchange rate replaced the fixed exchange rate that had been in place for years, and many tourism sectors felt the effect. For example, foreign liabilities rose because the fixed exchange rate policies reduced foreign exchange reserves. Tourism demand gained an incoming status (that is, foreign assets) after the execution of the decree of devaluation and the adoption of a floating foreign exchange policy. Thus, Turkish lira—which gained an artificial, unsound value against foreign monetary units due to the fixed foreign exchange policies—gained status after the devaluation and the floating exchange rate policy. That naturally restricted the demand toward foreign tourism, but it increased foreign visitors' preferences toward visiting Turkey.

Economic policies in a certain country closely influence tourism demands. Devaluation and monetary policies, structural quality of the sector, and high inflation all contribute to economic crises (Küçükaltan, 50–53). The economic policies may be listed as follows:

a.   Increase in prices (due to the inflation of demand) lead to increase in the prices for tourism goods and services. This poses a danger for domestic tourism demand, especially, because the real prices and expenses of tourism consumption decrease commensurate with increases in prices for tourism goods and services.

b.   Entry prices used for the production of tourism goods and services are influenced by cost inflation.

c.   Deterioration in the quality of goods and services due to high inflation may lead to tourists' discontent.

d.   Seasonality of tourism causes lack of employment in the sector.

Economic crises bring about a series of new problems for micro- and macro-sized sectors. The negative effects of crises on tourism businesses are shown in Table 2:

A devaluation policy employed by a government during an economic crisis may cause tourism to have a positive effect on a national economy. For example, the devaluation in Turkey during the 2001 crisis resulted in a net contribution of 6.5 billion dollars to the national economy the same year.

When adequate measures are not taken, an economic crisis can turn into a social problem, known as "social explosion" or "social crisis" (See 1.2.6. Social Crises).

Table 2: Possible Negative Effects on Tourism Businesses Caused by Crises [*]

Type of Effect	Explanation
Reduction in Demand	• Reservations may be canceled.
	• Market share may decrease.
	• Commission revenues may decrease; expected sales levels may not be met.
Costs	• Finance cost may rise.
	• Costs of products and service may rise.
Expenses	• Rent, personnel, energy, and communications costs may increase.
	• There may be damage and loss to buildings and equipment.
Financial Structure	• There may be difficulty in finding a foreign source of financing.
	• Auto-finance cannot be ensured.
	• There may be a liquidity risk.
	• Equity capital may lessen.
	• There may be difficulties in collecting receivables, or receivables may never be collected.
	• It may be necessary to pay for indemnity.
	• It may be necessary to dispose of fixed assets.
Weakening of Competition	• It may be more difficult to compete.
	• Market share may lessen.

Table 2: Possible Negative Effects on Tourism Businesses Caused by Crises (Continued)[*]

Type of Effect	Explanation
Influence on Employees	• Absenteeism and turnover of employees may increase.
	• The level of stress may rise.
	• Efficiency may decrease.
	• There may be physical casualties and deaths.
Administrative Effects	• There may be difficulties making sound decisions.
	• There may be no resources to solve problems.
	• The organizational climate may deteriorate.
	• It may be necessary to persuading the holding-group management on which one is dependent.
External Relations	• Relationships with creditors and members of the distribution channel may deteriorate.
	• There may be image problems.
Internal Relations	• There may be conflicts among employees.
	• Conflicts may occur between employees and the administration.
	• There may be interorganizational conflicts.
Decrease in Service Quality	• A decrease in service quality may increase customer complaints.
	• There may be a lack of market share.

[*]   **Resource:** Tanrısevdi, A. (July–September 2004): "Yönetici Bakışı İle Seyahat Acentalarında Dışsal Kaynaklı Kriz Olgusu," *Seyahat ve Otel İşletmeciliği Dergisi*, Year: 1, Vol: 1, p.39–40.

1.2.2. Political Crises

Political crises, which are defined as "political instability" (weakening of central authority's administrative power), may be classified as loss of authority that stems from the change of political authority, chaos in the election process, domestic affairs, and international tensions and wars.

Political crises are seen in underdeveloped and developing countries. Democracy cannot work within the rules and institutions of these countries and this comprises social crises, which also are known as social explosions (See 1.2.6. Social Crises).

Social crises cause economic problems. Economic bottlenecks occur as social crises deter new investments and thus reduce employment; this triggers new crises in domestic sectors. Tourism, which has a high demand elasticity, is first among the sectors that are most affected by the economic bottleneck.

The Balkans War (1992–1995) caused damage to Turkey's E-5 highway, which then decreased the number of tourists who entered the country by highway. That, in turn, damaged the economy of border cities such as Edirne.

The first Gulf crisis, which started with Iraq's invasion of Kuwait and subsequently led to the Gulf War, had negative repercussions on international tourism traffic. World tourism, which grew by about 4 percent each year until that time, grew only 1.2 percent in 1991.

Political crises occur most often in the Middle East, but these crises cause negative repercussions in adjacent countries too. According to data from the Turkish Republic Amman Embassy, Consultancy of Commerce, the number of tourists in Jordan decreased by 18 percent, from 140,252 to 114,560, in September 2001, as compared to September of the previous year. The Israeli-Palestinian conflict that started in September 2000 surely is most responsible for this drop in tourism (www.dtm.gov.tr/pazaragiris/ulkeler/urd).

Despite these world events, there was no decrease in the number of tourists visiting Turkey in 1991, but there was increased demand (up by 159,000 tourists) due to the reduced cost of tourism products made in Turkey (Kahraman 2003).

Although there was not a sharp decrease in national tourism demand, the Gulf War negatively impacted Central Asian businesses, especially airline companies. Iraq Airways and Kuwait Airways canceled their flights, and the number of flights to the Gulf from nearby countries decreased; fewer flights were scheduled from other countries, and the aircraft used was of a smaller capacity.

The political crisis in Central Asia after the Gulf War was a military act against Afghanistan. Kabul, the capital of Afghanistan; Kandahar, the headquarters of Osama bin Laden; and Herat, the city on the border of Celalabad and Iran, were struck by air bombing, led by the United States and aided by British forces. The operation used B-1, B-2, and B-3-type heavy bombing aircraft, hunter aircraft, and cruise missiles. According to the World Tourism Organization (WTO), international travel in South Asia dropped by 6 percent, due to the October 2001 conflict in Afghanistan (www.world-tourism.org/francais/newsroom/Releases).

The three-week military operation in Iraq, led by the United States with Britain's aid, on March 20, 2003, negatively affected not only the economy of the region but also the global economy. The tourism sector suffered the most from this act. Alain Feutré, head of the International Association of Hotels and Restaurants, headquartered in Paris, stated that there was a major decrease in hotel reservations in Paris and Berlin (www.turizimdebusabah.com/devam_popup.asp).

International tour operators began looking for ways to move beyond the bottleneck and economic recession caused by the U.S. invasion of Iraq. One solution was to offer major discounts off catalog prices. The large tour operators, like Touristik Union International (TUI), organized new campaigns, such as the "discount sales system." Additional discounts of 40 percent were offered, and economic package tours also were offered as an incentive in an attempt to fill vacant hotel beds and airline seats.

Civil aviation also was affected by the war in Iraq. The annual real growth in aviation (7–10 percent) instead fell by 12 percent. This parameter indicates that there were 19–22 percent fewer passengers between March and April 2003.

Political crises occur not only in the form of hot events but also in international diplomacy. The approval of the Armenian draft bill, for example, which was approved by the French senate on November 7, 2000, and by a large majority in the French national assembly and French president Jacques Chirac on January 18, 2001, caused a serious crisis in Turkey-France relations.

German tour operators excluded Israel from belief tour programs (travels for religious beliefs) due to the increasing tension between Israel and Palestine, instead including those Mediterranean countries (such as Egypt, Tunisia, and Turkey) that had alternative cultural potential.

War and political struggle often affect citizens and tourists, as they become inadvertent targets of guns and other weaponry. The main acts within this framework are as follows (http://arsiv3.hurriyet.com.tr/yazarlar/yazar/0,):

- On October 18, 1965, a Boeing Stratoliner aircraft belonging to the International Control Commission was the target of gunfire as it took off from Vientiane, Laos. Thirteen people were killed in the event.

- On September 3, 1978, an SA-7 missile struck a Viscount aircraft belonging to Air Rhodesia as it took off from Kariba, Zimbabwe. 34 passengers were killed during the landing, but 10 more later were killed by those who shot down the airliner.

- On February 12, 1979, soldiers of the Zimbabwe People's Revolution Army fired an SA-7 missile at a Viscount aircraft belonging to Air Rhodesia after it took off from the Kariba airport with its fifty-nine passengers and crew members.

- On September 4, 1985, a missile struck an AN26 aircraft belonging to Bakhtar Afghan Airlines a short time after it had taken off from the Kandahar airport. Fifty-two people, including five crew members, were killed in the crash.

- On August 16, 1986, the Sudan People's Liberation Movement fired an SA-7 missile at a Fokker F27 aircraft belonging to Sudan Airlines. Sixty people, including three crew members, were on board.

- On June 11, 1987, rioters fired a missile at an AN26 aircraft belonging to the Bakhtar Alwatana company as it took off from the Kandahar airport, headed for Kabul with its fifty-five passengers.

- On September 22, 1993, a missile hit a TU-154B aircraft belonging to Orbi Georgian Airlines as it was landing at the Sukhumi-Babushsra airport. Six of the twelve crew members and one hundred of the 120 passengers were killed in the event.

The most striking examples of political crises are changes in a country's government, such as those that occurred in Gürcistan in January 2004, in Ukraine in December 2004, in Özbekistan in May 2005 and Kirgizistan in September 2005

The tension began before the November 6, 2005, general elections in Azerbaijan are another example. The events that took place, described as a political crisis by some media, put the claims of military coup on the national agenda. President Aliyev tried to overcome the crisis with a cabinet reshuffle.

The biggest political crisis among developed countries at the start of the twenty-first century occurred in Germany. After the early general election held on September 18, 2005, the future of the grand coalition, which was to be formed by Social Democrats and the Christian Social Union, was placed at risk. The crisis leadership by Social Democrats and the ensuing statement by Edmund Stoiber, chairman of Christian Social Union and minister-president of Bavaria, indicating that he would not take part in the new government, served to increase suspicion of the new government. This was the point at which Germany's political crisis reached its peak.

As many political crises bring about social crises. This topic is dealt with in depth under the heading of "social crises."

Regardless of whether it occurs within domestic borders, a war (a type of political crisis) generally has religious, ideological, and/or economic causes. War has a negative effect on national tourism, although there may be a demand boom, resulting from nostalgia for the country at war. A demand boom also is possible in parallel with improvements in international relations.

The most fascinating example is the Battle of Çanakkale, which took place in 1915. Grandchildren of ANZAC (Australian and New Zealand Army Corps) soldiers visit the place where their elders fought against the Turkish army, commanded by Mustafa Kemal. They hold national and religious ceremonies in Anzac Cove, Gallipoli Peninsula, every year in April; this causes an immense tourism demand by thousands of Australian, English, and New Zealand visitors to Çanakkale.

Although this progress can be considered to boost tourism in the long run, political crises, in general, have negative repercussions on tourism, as well as negatively affecting other economic sectors in the short run.

1.2.3. Crises Due to Natural Disasters

Natural disasters, such as earthquakes, volcanic eruptions, tsunamis, floods, cyclones, and hurricanes, cause economic crises, yet they also may bring about political crises.

Although crises due to natural disasters cause economic problems in the short run, they may ensure a revival in some sectors, such as construction. A revival in the tourism sector, however, takes longer to evolve.

Turkey's magnitude 7.4 earthquake in Marmara in August 1999, and magnitude 7.2 earthquake in Bolu-Düzce on November 12, 1999, are the most obvious examples of crises in the tourism sector. The Marmara earthquake occurred at the height of the tourist season and caused approximately twenty thousand deaths and extensive material damage. After the Marmara quake, tourism agencies announced that half of their existing reservations had been cancelled; approximately 135,000 tourists decided not to travel to Turkey.

The Indian Ocean earthquake on December 26, 2004, also largely affected tourism. The epicenter of the magnitude 8.9 quake was Phuket, Thailand, and the Sumatra Islands. The tsunami that struck on December 26 killed more than 120,000 people around Indonesia, Thailand, the Philippines, Sri Lanka, and the Maldives, and ravaged Southern India, causing excessive material loss.

In Thailand, tourism is 12.2 percent of the gross domestic product (GDP), and tourism accounts for 9 percent of all employment. The tsunami caused a death toll of three thousand people, as well as twenty billion bahts ($510 million) in economic loss. After the tsunami, twenty thousand overnight stays were canceled, the occupancy rate at hotels decreased by 15 percent, and Phuket, which holds $1.8 billion of annual tourism income, lost $10 million dollars per day (www.linternante.com).

Twenty-three thousand people lost their lives in the tsunami disaster in Sri Lanka, where 20 percent of the gross domestic product is tourism. In the Maldives, a country of nearly twelve hundred coral islands, 71.4 percent of the economy and 64 percent of all employment is dependent on tourism. Twenty of the eighty-two tourism facilities were destroyed and the rest were badly damaged. It was calculated that the total insured damage in the Maldives was at $1 billion.

Floods and tornadoes also cause crises where they occur, including in Europe. The monsoon rains of late July 2005, which caused the heaviest flood ever recorded in the last century, and the landslide that killed 850 people in India caused a decrease in tourism demand.

A medium-intensity tornado occurred in Birmingham, England, in July 2005, injuring twelve people, three of them seriously. The crisis occurred during the tourism season; a state of emergency was declared immediately.

Hurricane Katrina hit the Gulf of Mexico in the United States on August 26, 2005, seriously impacting New Orleans, Louisiana, a city known primarily for its cultural and tourist features; in fact, 45 percent of New Orleans' population is made up of tourists. The state of Mississippi was most affected by the hurricane, however, as it sustained an insured damage of $100 billion. Hurricane Katrina, whose wind speed was near 300 kilometers per hour, hit the states of Louisiana, Mississippi, and Alabama. According to official figures, 241 people died and more than 270,000 people remain homeless.

Hurricane Wilma, which occurred on October 20, 2005, was most destructive in the Yucatán Peninsula and caused thirteen deaths in the Caribbean. While the Cancun coast of Mexico was underwater, the major damage occurred on the island of Cozumel. Many tourists in the holiday resorts were unable to leave and were stranded in the dark without water. Nine airports, including Miami International Airport, were closed because of the hurricane.

North America is familiar with natural disasters: in 1992 Hurricane Andrew hit southern Florida, killing forty-three people. Hurricane Andrew, which struck the Miami area, was recorded as "the most destructive hurricane in America" with an insured damage of $31 billion.

Experts who attended the second annual meeting of the Science and Technology in Society (STS) Forum, held in Kyoto, Japan, in September 2005, pointed out that the number of natural disasters increases constantly. Scientists stated that 400 natural disasters occurred between 1900 and 1940; 650 disasters occurred between 1960 and 1970; 2000 disasters occurred between 1980 and 1990, and 2800 disasters occurred between 1990 and 2000 (http://forum.mezun.com/forum/messageview.cfm?catid). These data demonstrate the level of the crises and the threat to tourism due to natural disasters.

1.2.4. Ecological Crises

Ecological crisis, defined as "depression resulting from the sudden occurrence of an ecological problem whose emergence takes a long while in a certain country," became a critical issue, particularly in the second half of the twentieth century. The main types of ecological crises are desertification, global warming, acid rain, toxic waste, inorganic vegetable production, damage to the environment as a result of industrialization, animal waste (which may cause mad cow disease, hoof and mouth disease, or avian influenza/"bird flu"), water pollution, and damage to plants and animals.

Ecological crises have a negative effect on the agricultural and tourism sectors, and economic crises occur because agriculture and tourism exploit nature itself.

This situation causes problems in other sectors, national and global economic problems in particular. It was reported, for example, that the daily loss to the Turkish Poultry Farming Association was 1.5 million Turkish liras after avian flu was detected in Kızıksa-Manyas, Balıkesir, in October 2005. Subsequent cases were detected in Asia and Europe; the flu killed one person in Indonesia. The European Commission prevented importation of winged animals from Croatia because avian flu was detected in that country. Later cases of the flu, which experts referred to as "the second wave," increased in China and Russia; more than sixty people lost their lives.

In October 2005 health ministers from thirty countries met in Ottawa, Canada, to discuss measures for dealing with avian flu. Developed countries took extra precautions and increased legal sanctions for minimizing pollution in natural resources, initially in water resources, to help stem this threat. France imposed various sanctions on the River Seine water basins, intended to reach a healthy ecological structure of water resources by 2015 (Miserey, 12).

The World Wildlife Fund announced the current results of global warming, based on a research carried out at England's Oxford University: a climate change has taken place at the Poles, with a temperature increase of two degrees. This climate change has the potential to harm Mediterranean economies, particularly agriculture and tourism by the year 2060 (www.cnnturk.com/BİLİM_TEKNOLOJİ/haber_detay.asp?). 30 percent of the world's tourism is in the Mediterranean basin. The effects of climate change due to global warming will differ with regard to time and place in the future, as it has changed in the past and continues to do so in the present day (Türkeş, 70–77).

Although ecological crises negatively impacts tourism, unbounded development in the tourism sector cause ecological crises. Before areas are opened to tourism, there must be regional planning and consideration of the physical capacity of a particular area. Ecological crises and tourism are mutually interactive.

Desertification, another factor of ecological crises, also will have a negative influence on tourism. The Mediterranean and Aegean regions can be presumed to be more open to the future desertification than other regions, due to the high topography of these regions, inappropriate use of agricultural lands, and other natural and manmade factors (Türkeş 1999). The tourism potential of these two regions is at high risk.

1.2.5. Biological Crises

Biological crises (biological war or biological terrorism) are the intentional utilization of microorganisms and their toxins, designed to harm people, domestic animals, and vegetation, and to damage production (www. dumlupinar.edu.tr/tr/ssa/biyolojik.htm).

Turkish Ministry of Internal Affairs, Directorate General of Civil Defense, produced a circular titled "Biological War and Protection Measures," in which the general features of biological warfare were explained as follows:

• Production of biological warfare weapons is easy and cheap.

- Biological warfare weapons are resistant to exterior conditions.

- They easily cause infection, disease, and epidemic.

- They can enter the body in various ways.

- The incubation period is short.

- Diagnosis and treatment of the diseases caused by biological weapons is difficult and takes a long time.

- Biological warfare weapons are fatal.

Biological crises—also defined as the utilization of bacteria and viruses that can cause serious diseases and death—have been more pronounced in the second half of the twentieth century, thanks to improvements in genetic engineering.

The term "biological warfare" often is mentioned together with "chemical warfare." Turkish Ministry of Health's circular, "The Methods of Protection and Treatment against Chemical and Biological Warfare Agents," affirms this point. Biological crises can be assessed with chemical crises.

The most extreme biological crisis of the twentieth century occurred during the Iraq-Iran War: Iraq used chemical weapons in Halabja and killed 5,000 people, mostly women and children. Emigration after the war had a negative influence on the economy in Turkey and Iran.

In 2001, U.S. Senator Tom Daschle received a letter containing anthrax. More than thirty U.S. senate employers were diagnosed with anthrax inhalation as a result, and the U.S. House of Representatives halted work for one week as a security measure. Anthrax cases first appeared in Florida and New York but spread in this way to Washington, D.C.

The threat of anthrax may appear trivial, however, in comparison to certain bacteria and viruses: the Ebola virus, bubonic plague, and salmonella are considered to be more dangerous than anthrax. The U.S. CIA and other Western information services possess various bacteria and viruses that can cause death by serious infection (Sayın, www.biyotek.com.tr/

makale/sayı16/biyolojikvekimyasalsavaş.doc.). It is possible to kill millions of people by biological warfare within a month.

Scientific research from the United States suggests that biological crises could increase through various foods, including milk. In response, the American National Science Academy distributed the article "Analyzing a Bioterror Attack on the Food Supply: the Case of Botulinum Toxin in Milk," published by Lawrence M. Wein and Yifan Liu, scholars at California's Stanford University (www.terrorisme.net/p/article_166.shtml).

Severe acute respiratory syndrome (SARS) caused a twenty-first-century global crisis. The SARS virus first appeared on February 26, 2003, in Hanoi, China, and quickly spread to international travelers. The World Health Organization (WHO) declared that 2,960 cases were seen between February 26, 2003, and April 12, 2003; 1,425 cases were treated; and 119 cases resulted in death (www.bilkent.edu.tr/~bilheal/aykonu/Ay2003/may03). SARS, which spreads via coughing, can spread rapidly.

SARS had negative effects on the global economy. Analysts at Morgan Stanley, an international investment firm, noted that the growth rate in West Asia decreased from 5.1 to 4.5 percent after the SARS epidemic (Pomonti, 12).

Data from the International Labor Office in Washington, D.C., notes that the employment rate in travel and tourism sectors decreased by 30 percent in the areas directly affected by the SARS virus (e.g., China, Hong Kong, Singapore, Taiwan, and Vietnam) and by 15 percent in neighboring countries such as Australia, Indonesia, Malaysia, New Zealand, the Philippines, and Thailand (Belau, 2).

When SARS cases appeared in downtown Toronto, Canada, a popular tourist area, the occupancy rates at hotels dropped by 30 to 40 percent; restaurants in the area saw a 20 to 30 percent decline in business. Prime Minister Jean Chrétien announced an advertising budget of ten million dollars to encourage visitors to come to Toronto, a necessary step after the negative effects of SARS on the national economy (Benkimoun, 11).

SARS also affected the aviation sector. Russia's Pulkovo Airlines canceled flights to Beijing as a consequence of the SARS threat. Turkish Airlines announced that passengers from Hong Kong, Bangkok, Singapore, Shanghai, or Beijing whose body temperature was more than 38 degrees Celsius (100.4 degrees Fahrenheit) would not be allowed to board its aircraft.

Swiss International Airlines canceled its flights to several international cities and decreased the number of flights to many others because of the SARS threat. Garuda Indonesia announced that the number of its passengers decreased by 20 percent in the first days after SARS appeared.

Four major hotels in Shanghai, China's largest city, were closed for three months due to the SARS outbreak. The Turkish Ministry of Foreign Affairs advised that citizens not travel to the People's Republic of China, Hong Kong, Taiwan, Singapore, Vietnam, the Philippines, Indonesia, or Thailand, except in cases of emergency.

In addition to its affecting the economy, SARS also caused political repercussions. Zhang Wenkang, former minister of health in China, resigned as a consequence of lack of success against SARS. The ministers of health of Asian countries held a meeting in Kuala Lumpur, Malaysia, and decided to employ strict controls of passengers at the airports and seaports. In Greece, the ministry of health chose to extend Easter holiday in schools because of Sars.

1.2.6. Social Crises

Economic and political crises may lead to a number of social crises. If people think that the political authority is inadequate or incompetent with regard to developing strategies to end crises, then "civil commotions" may occur.

Social crises, therefore, are not the reasons for but the results of other crises, particularly economic and political crises. Social crises may be defined as the illegal reactions of the people against the emerging crises, due to wrongful implication of the government and its inadequate efforts for the solution.

Unsolved economic and political problems often cause social crises. Economic problems, especially, trigger other crises. It is imperative, therefore, to solve the economic problem or change the economic situation, and to equip employers with more vocational skills in an attempt to remove possible conditions that may cause social crises (Mayer & Forest, 21).

A multidimensional example of the correlation between economic and social crises was seen in Argentina in 2001. Many people who found the International Monetary Fund's structural adjustment program oppressive chose to loot supermarkets and malls. Many armed conflicts occurred in the country, and the resignation of the minister of economy was demanded.

The crises in Argentina signaled a social crisis for other countries with economic problems, like Turkey.

'Sole 24 Orean' an Italian economy-finance newspaper stated that growing unemployment, currency leakage (transfer of the money to the external region), and hyperinflation indicated a social crisis in Turkey (www.ilsole24ore.com).

In Nairobi, Kenya, hundreds of people took to the streets on July 21, 2005, because its parliament had discussed changes to its constitution. The people who protested these changes—which included extending President Mwai Kibaki's authority—fought with the police and looted the shops; one protester was killed on the third day of the conflict.

Social crises also have followed political crises in other countries.

In November 2003, protesters forced Georgian president Eduard Shevardnadze to resign. Mikhail Saakashvili, leader of the National Movement, claimed that there had been vote fraud in the elections; he started a rebellion with about five thousand demonstrators. The European Union (EU), the European Parliament, and the European Council supported these claims, and one hundred thousand opponents protested the opening of the new parliament on November 22.

The presidential election, in which Mikhail Saakashvili was the only candidate, was held on January 4. This civil coup d'etat was recognized by the United States and the EU and became an indicator of how political crises can trigger social crises.

The social crisis in Ukraine started with the presidential elections in October 2004. None of the candidates received more than 50 percent of the vote, so a second vote was taken. According to official results, Viktor Yanukovych won the election, but his opponent, Viktor Yushchenko, and his supporters, as well as the United States and other Western countries, denounced the election, saying it as rigged. Widespread acts of civil disobedience initiated by the supporters of Yushchenko became known as the "Orange Revolution" because the demonstrators wore orange costumes. The Ukraine Supreme Court annulled the results of the first election and ordered a second round of voting. This time, Yushchenko won the election.

The political crisis in Kyrgyzstan began with the claim that the February 2005 elections were rigged and ended with the overthrow of President Askar Akayev in March 2005. Akayev's opponents, however, demanded a formal resignation, so as to remove any political uncertainty. These opponents obtained control in Osh, the second largest city in Kyrgyzstan and besieged on the presidential building in Bishkek after the demonstrations against Akayev.

After Akayev was overthrown, most cities in Kyrgyzstan, including Bishkek, were looted; fifteen people lost their lives. Overthrown-president Akayev initially would not agree to offer his resignation, so the political crisis in the country continued until he formally resigned.

Tension in Uzbekistan, which started with the trial of twenty-three people for radicalism, threw the country in rebellion. On May 12, 2005, hundreds of people invaded a prison in Andican and set free two thousand prisoners. The rebellion spread throughout the city, and by morning, nearly fifty thousand demonstrators demanded the resignation of President Islam Kerimov, in protest of living conditions and poverty. Later that day, army and police snipers opened fire from the rooftops; nine people were killed and thirty-four were injured.

Social crises frequently occur in underdeveloped and developing countries, where democracy is not thoroughly entrenched in all its institutions and regulations. The situation in developed countries, including the European countries, is contrary to this, because political and cultural conventions in the European countries are based on similar systems in the aspect of outer appearance, although they differ in function (Lavenir, 8).

Social crises may cause chaos in a society, as far as they are affected by internal and external factors. All social crises, however, is not due to resistance of public opinion against government policies. In Spain, for example, people demonstrated against the terrorist actions of the ETA (*Euskadi ta Askatasuna*, which translates as "Basque Fatherland and Liberty"). A new social action plan, the "solidarity movement," was established (Neveu, 13).

1.2.7. Political Violence-based Crises (Terrorism)

Political violence-based crises should be separated from other political crises in distinction. Political crises express a chaos or uncertainty in the political medium, but the political violence-based crises express a kind of chaos that aims to physically destroy the unprotected people, while claiming to have an ideological viewpoint. This also can be designated as "terrorism."

The relationship between terrorism and tourism is presented in detail in the following chapter.

All the aforementioned types of crises are closely related to tourism; that is why the concept of "tourism crisis" has been put forth. For instance, Sönmez, Bahman, and Allen define the concept of "tourism crisis" as follows:

"Any event that has the ability to threaten the ongoing tourism activities and services, harm a touristic destination in terms of security, appeal, and comfort, influencing the opinions of the visitors about the destination negatively, and thus cause a decrease in the number of tourists and tourism income and engender a collapse in local travel and tourism industry and an interruption in sectoral activities" (Glaesser, 6–7).

While some crises may occur without any apparent effect on tourism, others directly affect it. Crises due to natural disasters, political crises, and ecological crises are examples of the crises that occur independently of tourism; political violence-based crises (terrorism) and economic crises are examples of the crises that directly affect tourism.

1.3. The Definition and Scope of Terrorism

It is difficult to offer an exact definition of terrorism. This challenge is due to the different interpretations of "terrorist," with regard to different viewpoints. For instance, in some countries a person who commits a terrorist action might be defined as a "terrorist," whereas the same person might be defined as a ""freedom fighter" in other countries. A terrorist has difficulty with social integration, and he or she also rejects certain life choices and uses violence to oppose and remove any prohibitions (Servier, 124).

A terrorist is sometimes seen as being equivalent to an anarchist. When the two are analyzed semantically, however, it becomes clear that they are different from one another. In the dictionary of the Turkish Language Association, "anarchy" is defined as "chaos and idleness," whereas "terror" is defined as "intimidation, killing, and making material injury, destruction, frightening, terrorizing."

On the other hand, "anarchism" comes from Greek, etymologically, and is a synthesis of "an-" meaning "not, without"; "arch-" meaning "chief, principal"; and a suffix "-ism," which forms nouns of action, state, condition and doctrine. Therefore, anarchism can be defined as "not provided with authorization and power."

Anarchy is the inability to enforce the laws, absence of the rule of law, lack of authority, being against the authority, defying the law, and chaos when de facto surpasses de jure (İlhan, 15).

Anarchy is different from terrorism because terrorism uses violence or threat of violence against civilians. Terrorism, in general, is "any act taken with extraordinary methods, including the use of force and violence, with the aim of influencing social and political structure" (Kelly & Mitchell, 283).

Terrorism also may be defined as "the name given to violent actions, from kidnapping to murder, which aim to intimidate" (Ergil, 1).

For English historian, Paul terrorism is "to consciously and calmly use violence or threat of violence against any kind of action with a political content" (Johnson, 15).

The UN secretary general has a broader definition: "terrorism is the sum of actions with the aim of intimidating the society, killing or harming civilians and non-combatant masses, ensuring rapprochement through violence, obstructing a government from taking action or forcing an international organization to stop an action" (Flükiger www.terrorisme.net/p/article_155.shtm).

The common thread in all these definitions is that each equates terror to violence. The concept of violence, however, should be emphasized carefully, as violence can be analyzed in two ways: violence based on anomy, and strategic violence (Gassin, 254). The former expresses the freedom to behave aggressively by instinct; the latter is seen in the "hyperterrorism" that Al-Qaeda employs in its actions.

The word "terror" expresses an atmosphere of chaos and confusion in a particular system. The atmosphere of chaos and confusion may lead to methods based on violence (e.g., radical religious terror, separatist terror), but it also may have an aspect without any relationship to violence (e.g., traffic terror, food terror, media terror, football terror). Whether or not it is based on violence, all of these types of terror types result because of problems with deficiencies in administration, education, and inspection.

Terrorism, however, is an ideological action that is based on violence and directly targets human beings. The difference, then, between terrorism and terror is that terrorism employs an organized and systematic strategy and makes use of terror as a method (Bozdemir, 526).

Terrorism, at the same time, is an asymmetrical war (Balencie, 7). The basic feature of the asymmetrical war is the fight of a weaker mass or army against a stronger mass or army, with different and extraordinary methods.

The characteristics of terrorism can be listed as follows (Alkan, 17–19):

- Terrorism is not an ideology, a doctrine, or a systematic idea; rather, it is a strategy.

- Terrorism divides the world into two parts—"good" and "bad"—and names itself as "good."

- Terrorism prepares a scenario that legitimizes terrorist actions.

- Terrorism promises victory and a new order in the future.

- Terrorism has a general political purpose.

- Terrorism is an organized action that offers an alternative to the state authority.

- Terrorism is a part of international politics; thus, it cannot survive without external support.

- Financial support is an indispensable requirement for terrorism. Therefore, robbery and arms traffic are the means of income for terrorism.

- Terrorist actions emerge with the aim of seeking justice, offering an order, establishing an independent state, or all of these aims, each with different weight.

- Terror emerges through conscious and intentional actions.

- Employment of violence becomes a purpose for terror in time. It causes weariness by spreading horror and fear. Terrorism is tyrannical, ruthless, exploitive, and irregular.

- Terrorism serves other powers.

- Terrorism creates and makes use of its own language.

- Terrorism starts, develops, and survives with propaganda. Terrorism itself is a propaganda tool.

- Terrorists try to convince their audiences to see and perceive the world through their eyes.

- Terrorists see themselves as having sensitivity and superior consciousness.

- Terrorist actions are not based on an objective reality but on a subjective interpretation of the world.

- Terrorist actions require an organized effort. All of these actions are not individual but group actions.

The concept of the terrorist has been defined rather frequently, but divergent viewpoints have appeared. Jonna Thompson defines terrorists as those who organize and employ terrorist actions, targeting civilians and noncombatant masses; she categorizes terrorists as murderers and participants of a conflict.

The UN secretary general proposed that terrorist actions should be taken under the title of war actions. Regarding this, J. Thompson claims that those who employ terrorist actions should be treated within the context of war-crime conventions (1907 Haye, 1949 Geneva Conventions and Additional Protocols of 1977). Contrary to this, a terrorist may be seen as a freedom fighter (Flükiger, www.terrorisme.net/p/article_155.shtm).

Terrorists are distinguished from other types of criminals as follows (Hoffman, 43):

- Terrorists are political in their aims.

- Terrorists threaten to use force or resort to violence.

- Terrorists design the action, for they have psychological repercussions beyond the immediate target.

- Terrorists are governed by an organization with a selective chain of command or conspiratorial cell structure.

The Gent Court of Belgium pointed out a divergent conception in the definition of the terrorist during the trial of Fehriye Erdal, a suspect in the Özdemir Sabancı murder in Turkey and a detainee in Belgium. According to the Gent Court, Fehriye Erdal cannot be sentenced in Belgium for an assassination that occurred in Turkey, as she used a "semi-automatic weapon" in the attack, and the use of such weapons is not covered by the Belgian counter-terrorism act. Therefore, the Court ruled that the suspect cannot be tried within the framework of the European Convention on the Suppression of Terrorism. The European Convention on the Suppression of Terrorism states that in order to consider an action as a "terrorist action," the crime must have been committed using a full automatic weapon.

The concepts of terrorism and terrorist clearly differ with regard to divergent points of view. Various officials have expressed a desire to redefine the concepts of terrorism and terrorist. For instance, Hilmi Özkök, chief of the Turkish general staff, has stated that a scientific commission must be set up in order to determine the international definition of terror.

Terrorism today is effective not only in antidemocratic countries but also in democratic countries, because terrorism is born and survives in democracy and exploits its law (Altuğ, 13).

Etymologically, the word "terror" originated from the Latin "terrar terrorism"/"terrorem," which means "shaking from fear." The word "terrorism," as it targets civilians or a state institution in general, was first used in the eighteenth century after the French Revolution, during the "Reign of Terror" (Le Régime de la Terreur, 1793–1794).

At that time, Robespierre, leader of Le Comité de Salut Public (Committee of Public Safety), was fighting against the opponents of the revolution.

He arrested and subsequently executed the opponents. At the National Convention in 1794, Robespierre stressed that the aim of the constitutional government was to protect the republic, good citizens, and the whole nation; the enemy of the people, he said, deserved to die.

The word "terror" ultimately came to have its present meaning: killing and murdering individuals through the actions targeted at noncombatants. The discourse has taken the word to the international arena.

During the "Order of Terrorism" in France, Jacobinism emerged along with modern terrorism. In politics, Jacobinism refers to "making people adopt an opinion or a target that is believed to be true and absolute, using force and violence." In the context of the French Revolution, a Jacobin referred to a member of the Jacobin Club (Scruton 237).

In France, the first country where the word terrorism was used in a political sense, it is posited that the chronology of terror should be analyzed in three groups (Cettina, 21):

1. **Extreme left-wing groups:** They believe the capitalistic system and imperialism should be removed:

    -   Direct action, depending on European terrorism, actions of extreme left-wing organizations in Europe
    -   Bombing, massacre
    -   Actions with wide repercussions: booby-trapped cars used against military air bases
    -   (Two people were killed and twenty were injured at Rhein-Main Air Base)
    -   1987: The leaders were caught and detained and the action ended

2. **Separatist groups:** They defend independence and autonomy in some parts of France. Some of them are:

- Basque Terror Organization ETA (Euskadi Ta Askatasuna), IK (*Iparretarrak*)/1973
- British: FLB (Front de Libération de la Bretagne): 1964, ARB (Armée Révolutionnaire Bretonne):1971.
- Corsican: FLNC (Front de Libération National de la Corse)

These terrorist organizations made several attacks in France. Their actions had widespread repercussions, although the actions resulted in minimum loss of life with respect to other actions.

3.   International Terrorism Organizations

- Cuban
- Armenian (ASALA)
- Palestinian (FLP)
- Algerian (GIA/FLN)
- Al-Qaeda

These terrorist organizations caused serious problems in public services in France. France, however, had not considered international terrorism as a national priority until 1985.

Terrorism policy in France has been a "sanctuary doctrine" since the 1980s. France must employ this sanctuary doctrine in order to be rescued from international terrorism. Police precautions and diplomatic relations will be simultaneously carried out, according to this doctrine (Shapiro et Bénédicte, 67).

J.M. Balencie defines terrorism that is not described as a conventional method of fighting or described as a terrorist act as follows: "A method of uncertainty, which has public, religious, sports, and symbolic civilian areas as its target and penetrates into modern societies, causing a small number of individuals to seek for a large number of victims and reflects the excitement and violence among survivors and viewers in the most extreme way to attract the public attention" (Balencie, 7).

Dr. Michael Walzer, political philosopher and professor at the Institute of Advanced Study, School of Social Science, Princeton University, developed a critical approach in his book *De la Guerre et du Terrorisme* (Walzer, 173). Walzer states that militants tend to involve in terrorist actions without attempting to use legal opportunities. Terrorism, he says, should be the last method a militant applies, only after all possibilities have been used.

Terrorism seems to stem from extreme poverty and global inequality. Walzer, however, believes that destitution and inequality are not valid reasons for nationalist terrorist actions. For instance, African Diaspora has never been a hotbed for terrorists in Africa, even though global inequality, for which West is the most responsible, is so strong there (Walzer, 173–174).

Most countries face national and/or global threats of chronic terrorism. After September 11, fighting global terrorism became a priority, and the lists of terrorist organizations have been expanded. For instance, the U.S. Foreign Affairs Ministry listed the PKK Separatist Terror Organisation, DHKP-C (Revolutionary People's Liberation Party), and the Turkish Hezbollah in its annual report on terrorism.

It probably is not possible, however, to eliminate threats of terrorism completely. Terrorism has international support in many countries. This support consists of weapons and ammunition supply and financial, logistical, or training support. Therefore, guerilla movements, extreme and separatist terrorist organizations, are present in many countries. The lifespan of these organizations and the scale of their actions depend on their international supporters' presence and power.

The United Nations' five strategies for fighting terrorism emphasized the importance of withdrawing state support. These five strategies are as follows (www.un.org/apps/newsFr/storyF.asp?NewsID=1007000Cr=Terorisme&Cr1=Annan):

1. Encourage disaffected groups to use other tactics.

2. Deny terrorists the means to carry out attacks.

3. Discourage states from supporting terrorists.

4. Increase state capacity to prevent terrorism.

5. Defend human rights against terrorism.

1.4. Main Types of Terrorism

Terror can be classified according to various types.

1.4.1. Types of Terrorism According to Its Aims

In light of terrorist acts that have occurred in the world thus far, the aims can be listed as follows:

a) Terrorism targeting a political regime: The aim of the radical terrorist organizations is to damage and destroy the state system and its unitary structure, as well as internal and foreign policies of the governments using means of violence. These organizations aim to give a message to the world that terrorist acts are based on radical Islam and racial discrimination.

b) State terror: At times, governments use methods similar to terrorist methods in response to terrorist acts. Here, the main purpose is to break political resistance against the government and prove the government's power. State terrorism can be defined as "violent actions of the state towards people or groups who resist state authority and attempt to overthrow the regime." The United States' attack on Fallujah in November 2004 is an example of state terrorism.

On December 21, 1988, a Pan Am aircraft was blown up as it flew over Lockerbie, Scotland. Known as the "Lockerbie air disaster," it killed 259 people. The Libyan government accepted responsibility for this action a couple of years later.

State terrorism increased during the Cold War in the countries where totalitarian regimes are dominant. In that period, the Capitalist bloc aimed to prevent socialism from spreading to the world, whereas Eastern bloc aimed to export it. Each bloc promoted terrorist acts of groups and organizations within the other bloc; thus, terrorist acts reinforced by states became widespread.

Global state terrorism targets not only people or groups in terrorist actions but also the states that directly support terrorism, the countries and regions that do not fight against terrorism, and potential supporters of terror (Aktan & Vural, 25).

Definition of state terrorism is controversial because a state may consider military operations against terrorist actions as necessary for domestic safety, whereas another state may consider those same operations as "state terrorism."

It is difficult to arrive at consensus on the concept of state terrorism—whether the movements of liberation should be considered within the extent of the terrorism, rather than due to the biased approach of the states that protect national interests and international balance (Kaya, 49–52). For instance, Israel accepted its military operations toward Palestine in May 2004 as a security procedure. The president of Grand National Assembly of Turkey (TBMM) evaluated those operations as "state terrorism"(www.tbmm.gov.tr/develop/owa/ tbmm_basin_aciklamalari_sd.aciklama?p1=5467). When Recep Tayyip Erdoğan, prime minister of the Turkish Republic, was asked whether Israel's attacks against Palestine might be considered "state terrorism," Erdoğan emphasized the existence of "state terrorism" by responding, "What else can you call it?"(www.byegm.gov.tr/ YAYINLARIMIZ/DIS-BASIN/2005/01/04×01×05htm).

1.4.2. Types of Terrorism According to the Fields of Practice

It is possible to classify types of terrorism, which is an aspect of psychological war, according to fields of practice:

- **National terrorism**: This is inside, politically violent actions against the state, without any support from outside the country. The car bomb released at the Alfred F. Murray Federal Building in April 1995 in Oklahoma City was an obvious example of national terrorism.

- **International Terrorism:** International terrorism involves groups or individuals from at least two countries, whose terrorist activities are foreign-based and/or directed by countries or groups outside the country. The September 11 attacks, the explosions on November 17, 2004, in Istanbul, and the bombing attacks on July 21, 2005, in London are some of the international terrorism acts.

Terrorist acts are attributed internationally when they:

- Are directed at foreigners and foreign targets

- Are reinforced by the governments or more than one state

- Affect political mechanisms of a foreign government or international organizations (Altuğ, 23)

Rapid developments in globalization have influenced the dimensions and methods of international terrorism. Thus, it is appropriate to define international terrorism as global terrorism. Global terrorism uses not only guns but also explosives, and chemical and biological warfare. Such a situation expands the boundaries of terrorism and makes difficult to catch terrorists. The September 11 attacks and subsequent international terrorist attacks can be considered as the apex of global terrorism.

1.4.3. Types of Terrorism According to the Methods of Practice

- **Individual terrorism:** Violent political actions that target individuals in order to send messages to national and international public opinion (e.g., the assassination of Abraham Lincoln, the assassination attempt on Pope John Paul II, etc.).

- **Organizational terrorism:** The concepts of "terror" and "organization," as defined by the Anti-Terror Law, Act No. 3713: Law to Fight Terrorism, are as follows:

Terrorism is any kind of act done by one or more persons belonging to an organization with the aim of changing the characteristics of the Republic as specified in the Constitution, its political, legal, social, secular and economic system, damaging the indivisible unity of the State with its territory and nation, endangering the existence of the Turkish State and Republic, weakening or destroying or seizing the authority of the State, eliminating fundamental rights and freedoms, or damaging the internal and external security of the State, public order or general health by means of pressure, force and violence, terror, intimidation, oppression or threat.

For the purposes of this law, an "organization" constitutes of two or more persons coming together for a common purpose.

The term "organization" also includes formations, associations, armed associations, gangs, or armed gangs, as described in the Turkish Penal Code and in the provisions of special laws.

An organization is a group with an organized structure, consisting of people who adopt the same ideology and are directed to the same target (www.antalya.pol.tr/index.php?option=com_content).

Therefore, organizational terrorism comprises a systematic, ideological, and intentional cooperation.

Organizational terrorism also can be defined as "any kind of violent action carried out by two or more people to reject state regime and its applications, to debilitate state authority and to give messages to national and/or international public opinion." Terrorist organizations that carried out terrorist actions in a grand scale include the attacks on Instanbul, the PKK/KontraGel (Separatist Terror Organisation), Al-Qaeda, IBDA-C (Great East Islamic Raiders Front), the IRA[1] (Irish Republican Army), and the Red Brigades.

In some of the countries, militia forces claim to fight against terrorist organizations. For instance, pro-regime, armed militia forces such as the Ulster Defense Association (UDA) and the Ulster Volunteer Force (UVF) were formed in North Ireland, where people die each week because of the terrorism of the IRA. These militia forces assume the role of a judge, police, and executer, and they mutilate, even execute, the criminals and expel them with threats (Goldring, 109). The UDA, the largest Protestant paramilitia force in North Ireland, has carried out several acts against the IRA, which fights to end the British dominance over the country.

---

1.   The IRA (Irish Republican Army) is a terrorist organization that dates back to the seventeenth century and fights to end British rule in Northern Ireland.

2

TERRORIST ACTIONS TARGETED AT TOURISM, A PILOT MODEL AND MEDIA

2.1. Definition and Scope of Tourism

Travel has been a part of people's lives for centuries; travel, in fact, dates back to antiquity. Individuals have used various means of travel, often as a consequence of migration or war. When horses and donkeys became used as transportation vehicles, people built inns and caravansaries as accommodations, without any commercial purpose. The inns and caravansaries might be considered the beginning of the hotel business. Indeed, these developments reflect the evolution of tourism.

Not every type of travel is a part of tourism because travel must meet certain requirements in order to have a touristic aspect. In historical ages, people traveled for religious, military, cultural, and economic reasons. For instance, the Crusades were considered religious travels in the Middle Ages, and the Renaissance activities caused a density of cultural travels. The Seljuk and Ottoman Empires stressed the importance of the construction of roads, bridges, inns, and caravansaries. Even though such construction was for military purposes, it is among the factors that encourage travel.

The Industrial Revolution was a turning point in the eighteenth and nineteenth centuries. The Industrial Revolution led to technological improvements and increased the frequency of travel. The rail excursion organized by Thomas Cook in 1841 formed the basis for today's tourism and ensured the realization of the model, "travels with touristic ends."

The word tourism comes from the French verb "tourner," which means "to turn, to rotate, and to surround." The first definitions of tourism stressed sightseeing and entertainment as its end, whereas more recent definitions focus on the economic dimension.

The UN Conference on International Travel and Tourism, held in Rome, Italy, in 1963, shed light on the matter of tourism and travel. The conference stressed the importance of two criteria: reason of travel and duration of stay (Py, 14). In line with these criteria, business travelers, political refugees, and people who simply pass through a country cannot be considered within the scope of tourism.

Further, visitors are divided into two groups in terms of the duration of stay. The first group is composed of "day trippers" and the second is composed of the visitors who stay at least one night. Visitors in the latter category might be considered "international tourists" (Py, 14).

The International Conference on Travel and Tourism Statistics, organized by the World Tourism Organization in Ottawa, Canada, in 1991, concluded that tourism referred to "travels of individuals to places outside their place of residence for a certain period of time, not more than one consecutive year, for leisure, business and other reasons."

Business travels of not more than one year can be considered within the scope of tourism. Business travels to the cities with economic potential, and when there is demand for products and services provided by tourism businesses in those cities, complies with the essence of tourism.

Apart from these data, however, tourism can be defined as "the sum of travel activities performed by individuals individually or as a group for more than twenty-four hours for curiosity, religion, pleasure, sports, recreation, education, health, leisure, culture but not for political and commercial ends utilizing institutions of tourism industry" (Başol, 231).

Another definition of tourism is "the sum of travels of people to places away from their place of residence and work and the activities, events and relations emanated from their temporary accommodation and demands for products and services from the tourism businesses there" (Toskay, 50).

All the people who participate in the act of travel cannot be considered as "tourists," and not every travel should be evaluated within the framework of tourism.

Therefore, the criteria for evaluating an act of travel within the framework of tourism can be determined as follows:

- Travel within the area of residence cannot be evaluated within the framework of tourism, as the primary condition for tourism is that a person should travel outside the place of residence.

- Travel should not bear economic purposes. People should not have direct purposes of saving money or spending less money where they travel. In other words, desire for spending money should not be restricted. According to this, business trips to fairs and exhibits and the travels of politicians and diplomats to foreign countries have touristic purposes and can be classified among the main types of tourism.

- Travel should include staying at the destination at least twenty-four hours. Spending at least one night at the destination is the difference between tourist and day tripper.

- Travel to a destination away from the place of residence is not adequate to be considered an act of tourism. A person should demand products and services of the tourism industry in the district or country and use the institutions of the tourism industry, directly or indirectly.

Accommodation facilities, touristic (nonscheduled) transportation companies, tour operators, travel agencies, and free shops are directly related to the tourism industry. Underlying the commercial activities of these businesses is the fact that their target mass is the tourists.

Canteens, cafés, restaurants, scheduled transportation companies, and stores whose target audience is local people are indirectly connected to the tourism industry. Using the products and services of these businesses, which directly or indirectly are related to the tourism industry, provides economic vitality, and completely complies with the definition of tourism.

2.2. Reasons for Touristic Travel

The act of traveling constitutes the essence of tourism demand. People's motives for travel relate to the types of tourism.

The number of people who travel internationally has increased in recent years. International travel will affect more than 7 percent of the world's population, if the gradual upward socioeconomic trend in the world continues. It can be suggested that the profile of tourism demand also will change, along with the rate of demand.

Factors that encourage people to travel can be listed as follows:

2.2.1. Holiday (Vacation) Factor

People regain, maintain, and protect their physical and mental health while on vacation (Toskay, 50). Vacation (holiday) tourism can be defined as "the sum of events and activities stemming from the demand for tourism products and services provided by tourism businesses in during vacations."

Vacation may include several tourism activities (e.g., going to the beach, skiing, and cultural tours). The type of vacation a person prefers is a matter of taste; thus, some people enjoy cultural tours, while others prefer a seaside holiday. Moreover, some people may consider "extreme sports," such as bungee jumping and paragliding, as a type of vacation.

Travel to destinations away from the place of residence, and vacation in line with events and relationships noted in the definition of tourism are considered the extent of tourism.

Vacation often is not limited to the use of only one travel accommodation. Travel agencies diversify their services with various accommodation options when preparing package tours, and individual tourists also enrich their travel programs with cultural tours and shopping options. Diversified travel motives have enlarged the concept of "vacation."

2.2.2. Economic Factors

Economic tourism, which is on the rise, can be defined as "business travels for commercial purposes and the demand for products and services of tourism businesses during the travels."

The main factors that increase international trade are rapid globalization, multiple functions of international economic integration, and liberalization of the Eastern Bloc countries, especially after 1990. The increase in international trade and the New World Order (According to some researchers, it is an atmosphere in which the world's trend comes under one pole after the collapse of the Union of Soviet Socialist Republics.) caused people, particularly business people, to travel more frequently. The Russian Federation, for example, has become a popular tourist spot.

Travel by business people, as well as bureaucrats, also results in the development of economic tourism. Moreover, international fairs and exhibitions, with their growing importance in commercial activities, play a considerable part in economic tourism. Additionally, shuttle trade should also be analyzed within the scope of economic tourism.

Shuttle trade is one of the most effective ways of getting foreign currency into a country. Shuttle trade—that is, "the activity in which individual entrepreneurs buy goods abroad and import them for resale in street markets or small shops"—has become a type of government-supported travel without customs restrictions.

In 1984, the Turkish government abolished visas for Greek citizens to encourage day trips, which increased shuttle trade. Shopping trips were organized from the Greek cities of Iskece, Gumulcine, and Dedeagac, all near the Turkey-Greece border, but after the complaints by local retailers, the Greek government restricted these economic travels to Turkey by adding extra bureaucratic procedure in customs.

The dissolution of the Soviet Union in 1990, however, was a milestone for shuttle trade. The liberation tendencies that began with the formation of new countries entering a free-market economy resulted in outgoing tourism with economic purposes. Laleli, Istanbul, has become a center for shuttle traders. As a consequence of demand, bed capacity at hotels has reached 30,000, and the number of the stores has grown to 25,000 in Laleli (Korkmaz, 2). Shuttle trade also is seen frequently in other districts, such as Beyazıt and Kapalıçarşı (Grand Bazaar) in Istanbul and in the cities close to the border, such as Edirne, Antalya, and Trabzon.

In line with these developments, the Turkish government encouraged shuttle trade when it published a value-added tax notification on March 1, 1997, which noted that the goods that shuttle traders purchase would be zero-rated for value-added tax. China, which saw the benefits of shuttle trade to the economy, has become an alternative market for shuttle traders in spite of its geographic remoteness.

Table 3 displays the amount of foreign currency that entered the Turkey via shuttle trade. A sharp decrease in shuttle trade income exists, as compared to 1996. One reason for that drop is that alternative countries like China, where labor cost is expensive, increased their share in the Russian market. Another reason is the influence of diplomatic problems between Turkey and Russia with regard to economic relations. Still, 1,605,259 Russian visitors traveled to Turkey in 2004.

Table 3: Shuttle Trade Incomes in Turkey (1996–2004) [*]

Years	Income (Millions $)
1996	8.842
1997	5.819
1998	3.689

Table 3: Shuttle Trade Incomes in Turkey (1996–2004) (Continued)[*]

Years	Income (Millions $)
1999	2.255
2000	2.944
2001	3.039
2002	4.065
2003	3.953
2004	3.880

[*]   **Resource:** www.muhasebat.gov.tr, August 18, 2005

2.2.3. Cultural Factors

Culture, also defined as "civilization," is a "set of learned beliefs, values, behaviors, customs, feelings, thoughts, language, art, and a way of life shared by the members of a society" (*Encyclopédie Larousse*, 134).

Tourism for cultural purposes or "cultural tourism" can be defined as "traveling to destinations away from the place of residence to see traces of a society's language, art, lifestyles, and values, which are based on the society's economic and political development."

Historical places, ruins, architecture, congresses, traditional cuisine, and religious heritage are among the factors that encourage people toward cultural tourism. It is difficult to determine, however, which factor has priority for tourists, as tourism products or services have an integrated structure, and products cannot be categorized or separated according to tourists' priorities.

Tourists who purchase a package tour automatically expect all tourism services (e.g., visiting historical sites, shopping, entertainment). Therefore, visiting historical sites cannot be directly accepted as a priority reason for travel for all tourists, except for groups with special interest. Because the number of tourists who travel for congresses or religious purposes easily can be determined, these activities can be viewed as "cultural factors."

2.2.3.1. Congress Tourism

Cultural improvement leads to sharing that cultural knowledge, which plays a considerable part in increasing congress tourism.

Congress tourism is "a set of organized travels to destinations away from the place of residence for collective meetings on various subjects." Congress tourists also benefit from other aspects of tourism, such as vacation or entertainment (Dalli, 15).

Research shows that congress tourists have high income levels, along with high cultural knowledge. Moreover, their expenses are paid by their employers or sponsors. Congress tourists contribute to local economy by shopping in their spare time.

A foreign tourist who comes to Turkey for a congress spends approximately two thousand dollars. This amount is three times more than the expenditure of a tourist who travels on holiday. In addition to their high income levels, congress tourists also are highly educated, intellectual and curious.

Istanbul, which is now a world city, attracts tourists' attention with its fifteen to twenty international congresses per year. Some important centers for congress, such as Amsterdam, Paris, Vienna, Copenhagen, and Sydney, organize approximately forty major congresses per year; the total number is over one thousand. Turkey's capacity for congress tourism seems inadequate.

Only the Aegean Region has a wide spectrum of products to serve congress tourism. Some meeting rooms in the hotels have a capacity for a few hundred people, but separate congress-conference halls for 4,000 to 5,000 people should be constructed (Varlier, www.esiad.org.tr/esiad.nsf/0/ 1E95E2B003672912C2256DB2004F062A?OpenDocument).

2.2.3.2. Culture Tourism

Travels that are organized to places with cultural features, with the aim of enjoying these features, constitute cultural tourism. Culture tourism includes travels to historical and religious places, museums, monuments, and ruins, as well as folkloric motives (food/drink, handcrafts, folk dances, etc.).

Tourists' demand for culture tourism has increased because tourists want to learn more about the culture of other countries or regions.

What matters here is how to classify travels to holy places and to decide whether these travels belong to culture tourism or faith tourism.

Research indicates that travels to Mecca, Medina, Jerusalem, and the Vatican—holy places with respect to celestial religions—can be categorized as "faith tourism." Other visits that aim to develop cultural knowledge, however, can be considered "culture tourism." Culture tourism also includes a Christian's visit to a mosque or a Jew's visit to a church or a Moslem's visit to synagogue, for the purposes of observation and getting information.

Therefore, the regions that succeed in protecting their cultural values and in advertising them earn a great amount of revenue from tourism. For instance, traditional vintage festivals (e.g., the Nice Carnival) and traditional religious days (e.g., Fête-Dieu ve Fête de Pénitents in Provence, Fête des Pardons in Bretagne) constitute international tourist attractions and meeting places for local people (Boret, 38).

People want to learn about the local cultures of the country or region they visit; they want to diversify the type of consumer culture imposed by globalization, as culture is one means of globalization. The first phase of culture is the dominance of monotonous consumer culture all around the world. This comes in the form of the dominance of international companies and/or international brands (Kongar, 26–27). Therefore, countries that manage to protect their culturally specific features from the dominance of globalization might increase their market share in future. These

days, countries take rapid action on this matter. Ministers of Culture and/
or representatives of forty-six European Council member countries discussed strategies for developing intercultural dialogue when they met at a
conference in Faro, Portugal. The resulting "Faro Declaration" stated that
national and local cultures must be supported against the dominance of
the global and transatlantic culture industry.

2.2.4. Other Factors

Other factors that cause people to travel for tourism purposes are as follows:

- Utilization of tourism products and services by sportsmen, managers, and spectators (sports factors)

- Utilization of tourism products and services during international
  visits by diplomats, politicians and bureaucrats (political factors)

- Utilization of alternative tourism products and services, such as
  extreme and adventure sports, such as rafting, paragliding, hiking
  (alternative factors)

- Utilization of tourism products and services for health purposes
  (e.g., thermal treatment, cave treatment.) by seniors (health factors)

Research indicates that international travel has risen and will continue to
rise. Figure 2 shows that the number of international arrivals—166 million people in 1970—will escalate to about 1.5 million people in 2020.

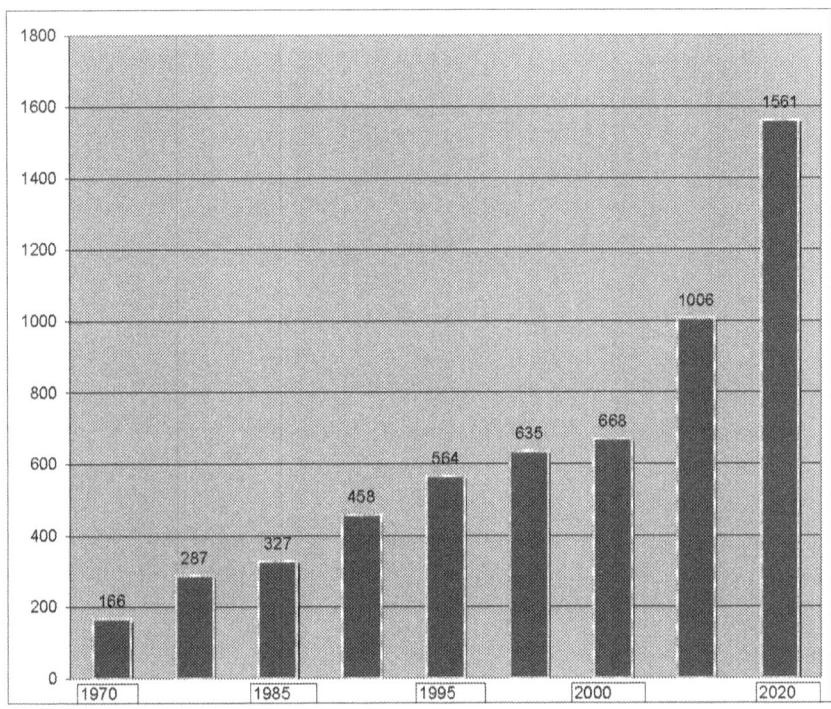

Figure 2: International Tourist Arrivals (Millions People, 1970–2020)
Resource: www.geotourweb.com, July 20, 2005

It is estimated that income from international tourism will rise in parallel with the rise of international tourism movements (Figure 3).

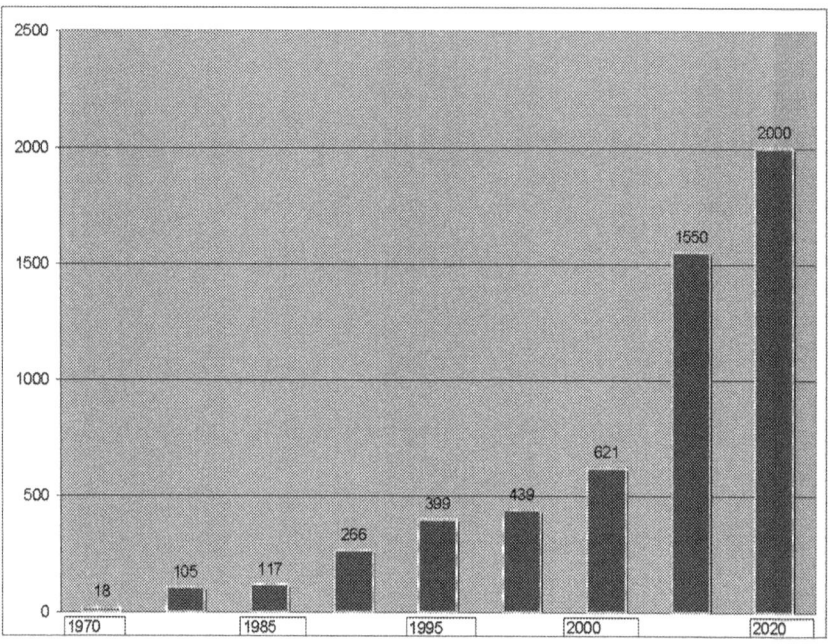

Figure 3: International Tourism Income (Billions Euro, 1970–2020)
Resource: www.geotourweb.com, July 20, 2005

Some factors that play a considerable role in the rise in the number of international tourists and tourism income are as follows:

- Tourism alternatives dependent on changes in individual's tastes and preferences have increased in number.

- Rapid improvements in mass communication and information technologies have been observed.

- Transportation services have been improved in terms of speed, safety, and comfort.

- Rapid globalization development increased economic, political, and cultural relationships; thus, types of tourism also have improved.

- International tourism companies, which grew in number and scale along with horizontal/vertical integration, attempted to increase their sales and market shares.

- After the 1990s, regional economic integration expanded and became more functional. The EU (European Union) and EFTA (European Free Trade Association) in Europe, NAFTA (North American Free Trade Agreement) and MERCOSUR (a treaty establishing a common market between Argentine, Brazil, Paraguay and Uruguay) in America, ASEAN (Association of Southeast Asian Nations) in Asia, and APEC (Asia Pacific Economic Cooperation) in the Asia-Pacific are examples of economic grouping. Citizens of member countries were provided with traveling facilities, and formalities at the frontier were reduced for them.

- Most of the countries perceived the importance of holiday tourism and its economic aspect; thus, macroscale dynamic marketing policies have been developed.

There has been a considerable increase in the number of factors that retard the demand in tourism, in parallel with the factors that increase the demand. Crises are foremost among these factors. Restrictions in travel brought about by crises, which were highly influential at the end of the twentieth century, are the major obstacles to tourism.

2.3. The Relationship Between Terrorism and Tourism

The threat of global terrorism has rapidly increased its impact on tourism all over the world. Global terrorism has used tourism, which is the most sensitive sector in globalization, as its target since the 1980s.

The only common point between tourism and terrorism is that both have defenseless people as their target audience. Tourism, a sector whose subjects are human, provides psychological and physiological comfort, focuses directly on humanism, grows in democratic and liberal environments, and ensures intercultural conciliation.

Terrorism, on the other hand, targets human life. It exploits violence and aims to intimidate, is based on intercultural differences and encourages these differences, and grows in antidemocratic environments.

Reasons for identifying terrorism with tourism are listed as follows:

- Terrorist actions that aim at tourism have immediate repercussions in the world public opinion, as tourism has an international aspect.
- It diminishes the public image of a country or an institution via tourism.
- It damages the economy of the target country via tourism, the multiplier effect of which is high.
- It creates an appropriate atmosphere for dialogue between the administrators of a target country and the victim citizens who carry out a terrorist act aimed at its own citizens.
- It creates an international diplomatic-crisis environment between the target and a third country, when an action toward the victims of the target country occurs in a third country.

Maslow's hierarchy of needs purports that safety needs are one level above physiological needs; safety is a fundamental concept that motivates human beings.

When Maslow's theory is interpreted within the concepts of tourism, safety is one of the most important factors that determine the destination preference of visitors. A feeling of safety in the preferred destination directly influences tourism demand and tourism incomes. A 1 percent increase in terrorist actions causes a 49 percent decrease in tourism income. There exists an inverse proportion of 5 percent between tourism income and terrorism (Emsen & Değer, 78).

2.4. The Concept of Tourist Terrorism

Terrorism gains an international quality, crossing national borders, due to the nationalities of the perpetrators, victims, and participants of the terrorist action (Fearey, 25). When terrorist acts are chronologically analyzed, it is clear that terrorism aims at foreign citizens, rather than at tourism businesses.

Terrorism has targeted foreign citizens since the 1970s. In the 1970s, the targets were chosen diplomats or athletes who represented a particular country; terrorism edged toward diplomatic and sports targets, along with military targets, in those years. The popularity of commercial targets began in the 1990s.

In 1972, Palestinian terrorists asked the Israeli government to release their friends from prison, and they killed eleven Israeli athletes and administrators at the Olympic Village during the Munich Olympics. The games were suspended for thirty-four hours because of this action. In 1996, an American and a Turkish national TV cameraman were killed in an explosion in the Olympic Park during the Atlanta Olympics.

A bomb that was planted in a car by the IRA exploded in a shopping center during the Europe Football Championship in Manchester, England, on June 15, 1996. Two hundred people were injured.

After such terrorist acts were carried out at sporting events, more attention was paid to security and more money was allocated for security measures. For instance, at the Salt Lake City Winter Olympics in 2002, $1.9 million were allocated for security due to the fear caused by the September 11 attacks (Collier, www.lemonde.fr/cgi-bin/ACHATS/acheter.cgi? offre= ARCHIVES&type_item-ART).

Several terrorist acts have been carried out against diplomatic agencies of certain countries. Some of the acts aimed at diplomatic targets are listed as follows:

- The revolutionary organization on November 17 in Greece first became known by its assassination of Richard Welch, an American diplomat, in December 1975. The organization has carried out approximately seventy armed and bomb attacks since 1975, aimed primarily at Greek, American, and Turkish diplomats.

- On April 18, 1983, sixty-three people, including seventeen Americans, were killed in a bomb attack on the American Embassy in Beirut.

- On September 20, 1984, sixteen people were killed in a bomb explosion in a building adjacent to the American Embassy in Beirut.
- On August 7, 1998, thousands of people injured and 224 were killed in bomb explosions at the American Embassies in Nairobi, Kenya, and Tanzania.

Major terrorist actions on military targets also have occurred. One of the most striking examples of these acts happened on October 23, 1983, when a Shiite suicide bomber attacked the barracks of the U.S. Naval Forces in Beirut, killing 241 naval officers.

The National Liberation Army, which was founded in Colombia in 1963, is known for its actions against foreigners. In 1970, the Egyptian al-Gama'at al-Islamiyya was founded by Shaykh Umar Abd Al-Harman. The organization aims to change the Egyptian regime and establish an Islamic order. Its number of militant members is uncertain, but it is known for its acts against tourists.

The People's Mojahedin Organization, founded in 1960 in Iran, is known for attacks on the Iran Embassies in thirteen countries and for the kidnapping of American citizens.

Turkey, surely, is a country that has suffered most from terrorism. The Armenian terrorist movement, which dates back to the 1890s, has committed terrorist actions aimed at Turkish diplomatic agencies since the 1970s. The Armenian terrorist organization ASALA (Armenian Secret Army for the Liberation of Armenia) carried out several attacks against Turkish diplomats in attempt to force the Turkish government to acknowledge its role in the Armenian genocide during World War I.

Table 4 lists the attacks against diplomats with a Turkish passport within the last twenty years:

Table 4: Terrorist Actions Targeted at Turkish Diplomatic Representatives (1973–1994) *

Date(month/day/year)	City/Occupation	Name
01.27.1973	Santa Barbara/Consul General Consul General	Mehmet Bayda Bahadır Demir
10.22.1975	Vienna/Ambassador	Danış Tunalıgil
10.24.1975	Paris/Ambassador Driver	İsmail Erez Talip Yener
02.16.1976	Beirut/Secretary General	Oktar Cırıt
06.09.1977	Vatican/Ambassador	Taha Carım
06.02.1978	Madrid/Ambassador's wife Retired Ambassador	Necla Kuneralp Besir Balcıoğlu
10.12.1979	La Hayes/Ambassador's son	Ahmet Benler
12.22.1979	Paris/Tourism Attaché	Yılmaz Çolpan
07.31.1980	Athens/Attaché Attaché's daughter	Galip Özmen Neslihan Özmen
12.17.1980	Sydney/Consul General Security Attaché	Sarik Arıyak Engin Sever
03.04.1981	Paris/Attaché Advisor	Reşat Moralı Tecelli Arı
06.09.1981	Geneva/Secretary	M.Savaş Yergüz
09.24.1981	Paris/Security Attaché	Cemal Özen
01.24.1982	Los Angeles/Consul General	Kemal Arıkan
04.08.1982	Ottawa/Honorary Consul General	Kani Güngör
05.04.1982 06.07.1982	Boston/Honorary Consul General Lisbon/Attaché	Orhan Gündüz Erkut Akbay
08.27.1982	Lisbon/Colonel-Military Attaché	Atilla Altıkat
09.09.1982	Bourgas/Attaché	Bora Süelkan

Table 4: Terrorist Actions Targeted at Turkish Diplomatic Representatives (1973–1994) (Continued)*

Date(month/day/year)	City/Occupation	Name
01.08.1983	Lisbon/Administrative Attache' wife, Nadide Akbay was wounded in the assassination of her spouse in 07/06/1982 and died in 08/01/1983.	Nadide Akbay
03.09.1983	Belgrade/Ambassador	Galip Balkar
07.14.1983	Brussels/Administrative Attaché	Dursun Aksoy
07.27.1983	Lisbon/Secretary General's wife	Cahide Mıhçıoğlu
04.28.1984	Tehran/Secretary's husband	Isik Yönder
06.20.1984	Vienna/Labor Attaché	Erdoğan Özen
11.19.1984	Vienna/International Officier internationnal	Enver Ergun
07.10.1991	Athens/Media Attaché	Çetin Görgü
12.11.1993	Baghdat/Administrative Attaché	Çağlar Yücel
07.04.1994	Athens/Secretary General	Haluk Sipahioğlu

*   **Resource:** The Chronlogy of Armenian Terrorism (La Chronologie du Terrorisme Arménien) www.tetedeturc.com, 04.01.2002

Terrorist acts against tourists began in 1994. One reason for this is that the tourists are more defenseless, as compared to diplomatic representatives who employ more security measures. They also travel in groups or individually, which creates a more convenient environment for terrorists.

"Tourist terrorism" is defined by some sociologists as terrorism that targets tourists who travel to a particular country (Cross, www.openair.org/cross/tour.html). The formalities at countries' borders, which were reduced with rapid developments in globalization, were increased after global terrorist actions against tourists. Many countries increased their security procedures at their frontiers. This situation points out that global terrorism is one of the main obstacles to the development of tourism.

Pizam and Fleischer focus on two aspects in determining the impact of terrorism on tourism demand (2001):

1. The intensity of terrorism in a particular country (the number of people killed and injured in terrorist actions)

2. The frequency of terrorist action in the country (the number of terrorist actions occurring within a particular period)

The intensity and frequency of terrorist actions in a particular country determines the tourists' preference for a destination. Chronic terrorism in a particular country influences tourism demand negatively, whereas a low frequency and low intensity of terrorist actions generally have no influence on the on preference for destination.

2.5. A Periodical Approach Toward Terrorist Acts Targeted at Tourism in the World, and September 11, 2001

Many sectors have suffered from global terrorism. The countries that have suffered most from global terrorism, however, are those with extensive tourism potential, due to the fact that terrorism causes the most damage through tourism. The only positive development caused by terrorism has been in defense sector (Morgil, 166).

Terrorist acts aimed at tourism can be chronologically analyzed in three periods: the Cold War period between 1945 and 1989; the period between 1990 and 2001, when U.S. president George W. Bush declared a New World Order; and the period that started with the attacks of September 11, 2001, which was accepted as a milestone for global terrorism.

First period: During the "Cold War period," the United States and the Soviet Union attempted to maintain their domination over the world. They also carried out military operations in the Middle East and in the countries with rich natural resources and strategic positions.

The acts of several terrorist organizations against tourists and the tourism businesses, which directly (accommodation facilities, tour guides, travel agencies) or indirectly (transportation services, entertainment facilities, catering companies) depend on tourism, started in the 1970s. The chronology of terrorist actions that directly targeted the tourism sector dates back to this time.

Terrorist actions that had a negative effect on tourism actually date back to 1946. A bomb explosion at the Roi David Hotel, Jerusalem, on July 22, 1946, killed 111 people and injured forty-six others. The fact that the attack occurred at the Roi David Hotel, however, which was protected by English forces at the time, proves that tourism was not a direct target. Terrorist actions directly targeted at tourism have been analyzed in this context.

Many terrorist actions that directly target tourism have occurred, with the aim of harming the national economy and tarnishing the image of a country. This situation is an obvious threat to the countries with rich tourism potential.

The terrorist action of the ETA[1] in Spain is an example of such a situation. The ETA has edged toward tourism facilities since 1984 and has carried out a series of bomb actions in the hotels on the Costa de Sol from 1985 to 1987.

The most significant terrorist actions against tourism in this period are chronologically listed as follows:

- The Abu Nidal terrorist organization, established on November 22, 1974, by two hundred Palestinians living in France, Italy, Spain,

---

1.   The Basque Separatist Movement was founded in 1962 by militants separating from the EKIN group. They assert that they fight for the freedom of the Basque region in Spain. During the Cold War, ETA enjoyed the support of Southern Yemen, Algeria, Libya, Lebanon, and Nicaragua, and had close relations with Italy's Red Brigades and the Palestinian groups. ETA receives the biggest support, however, from the Basques in France. ETA takes its place in the EU's list of terrorist organizations.

and Austria, attacked the Semiramis Hotel in Damascus in **September 1976**.

- Puerto Rican terrorists bombed a bar on Wall Street in New York City on **January 27, 1975.** Four people were killed and sixty were injured in the incident.

- Four terrorists of the Baader-Meinhof, a German terrorist organization, hijacked a Boeing 747 with its German passengers to Mogadishu in **1977.** The joint operation of an English–German counterterrorist team neutralized the terrorists before any of the hostages were harmed.

- An Air France flight was hijacked by terrorists (two Palestinians and two Baader-Meinhof members) during its Paris–Tel Aviv flight on **June 27, 1976** and forced its landing at Entebbe Airport in Uganda. The terrorists demanded that their friends be released from prison. There were 250 people among the passengers and flight crew; eighty-three of whom were Israeli. Jews were detained by the fully armed terrorists, but other passengers were released. Team operations saved the hostages, although two people lost their lives.

- An Egypt Airlines plane was hijacked by terrorists during its Athens-Cairo flight on **November 23, 1985**. Fifty-six of the passengers and two terrorists were killed in the incident. On December 27, 1985, fifteen people were killed in the attacks on El Al ticket windows at the Rome and Vienna airports.

- "Skinheads" (neo-Nazis) in Germany attacked foreigners, particularly Turks, in **1985**.

- An American passenger was killed by terrorists who hijacked an Egypt Airlines plane in **June 1985**. The plane landed on Malta, and sixty people lost their lives in the tragic rescue operation of the Egyptian commandos.

- **July 1985**: A TWA plane that was hijacked over the Mediterranean caused a hostage crisis that was to last for two weeks. The plane landed in various airports in different countries and finally, the hijackers released thirty-nine hostages in Damascus. In the same month, thirteen people, including six Americans, were killed in an armed attack in El Salvador, Central America.

- **December 1985**: Four Arabic suicide commandos carried out attacks at Rome and Vienna airports, aiming at American and Israeli passengers, and killed twenty people, including themselves.

- **April 1986**: Four people died in a TWA aircraft that exploded in air and made an emergency landing at Athens airport. In the same month, two people, including one American, were killed in another explosion that occurred in a nightclub in Berlin.

- Twenty-one people died in an attack on a Pan Am plane on **September 5, 1986**, in Karachi.

Second Period: The second period of terrorist actions against tourism is the 1990–2001 period, when the Soviet Union collapsed, and liberalization tendencies began and accelerated in the Eastern bloc countries. This period saw terrorist actions such as kidnapping and hijacking. Terrorism also edged toward commercial targets, in addition to the businesses that directly and indirectly depended on tourism.

For instance, Shining Path, a Maoist guerilla organization formed in the 1960s in Peru, increased its bomb attacks on tourism targets. Because of these incidents, the number of the foreign visitors dropped from 350 thousand in 1989 to thirty-three thousand in 1991 (www. geotourweb.com/nouvellepage12htm).

This period also hosted the marginal Islamist terrorism's demonstration of power. A bomb action targeted at the World Trade Center in New York in 1993 and carried out by Omar Abdul Rahman, nicknamed "the Blind Imam," is considered to be the first sign of global terrorism. Six people lost their lives in the attack, and the "Blind Imam," the perpetrator of the attack, was condemned to lifetime imprisonment.

In this period, the terrorist organization al-Gama'at al-Islamiyya increased its terrorist acts. It carried out 120 actions against tourists solely in Egypt between 1992 and 1995; thirteen tourists were killed.

Some of the terrorist actions of the second period are as follows:

- On **January 19, 1990,** two Swiss citizens who were members of Red Cross were killed and one Swiss citizen was injured by the militants of the Moro Islamic Liberation Front in Mindanao, the Philippines.

- On **February 8, 1990,** an American tourist was killed by the militants of the Shining Path (Sentier Lumineux) in Peru.

- On **March 2, 1990,** an American died and twenty-nine people, including fifteen Americans, were injured in an attack on a bar frequented by the Americans in Panama City.

- On **July 28, 1990,** a Canadian tourist died and twenty people were injured in a bomb attack in Tel Aviv.

- On **March 11, 1991,** Corsican liberation partisans planted explosives in a hotel in Calcatoggio.

- On **December 4, 1991,** IRA militants left a car bomb in front of the Hotel Europa. The hotel was severely damaged and a large number of people were injured in the incident.

- On **June 8, 1993,** two Egyptians died and eighteen tourists, including Americans and Syrians, were injured in a bomb attack on a tourist bus near the Gizeh pyramid.

- On **June 11, 1993,** a car bomb exploded in a parking lot of a hotel in Algeria. Three people died and three were injured in the attack.

- On **February 23, 1994,** a bomb exploded in a train in Asyut, Egypt. Six people (two New Zealanders, two Germans, and two Australians) were injured. The Armed Islamic Group claimed responsibility for the attack

- On **July 11, 1994,** an Italian tourist and a Greek were seriously injured in a bomb explosion at a restaurant in Rhodes, Greece.

- On **August 26, 1994,** a Spanish tourist died in an armed attack on a bus on the Luxor road.

- On **September 27, 1994,** two German and two Egyptian were killed in open fire in Hurghada, Egypt.

- On **October 23, 1994,** an English tourist died and three English tourists were injured in an attack in northern Egypt.

- On **January 15, 1995,** an American tourist was killed and his wife was injured in Kampuchea. The couple's tour guide also was killed in the attack.

- In **summer 1996,** the ETA carried out six bomb attacks in Costa Dorado. Hotels were damaged in the incident.

Two factors that formed a basis for the third period and triggered global terrorism first appeared in the second period:

1. Religious terrorism: Terrorist actions that were carried out with either extreme leftist tendencies or extreme rightist tendencies served a religious ideology in the 1990s. In addition to the Middle East terrorist actions, which also were called "radical Islamist terrorism," new terrorist organizations emerged, such as the Aum Sect in Japan. While no religious terrorist group existed in 1968, the number of the religious terrorist organizations by 1995 was twenty-six (Erkmen, 6).

The situation formed a basis for global terrorism, the process of global religious terrorism that was to start with the attacks of September 11, 2001. The fact that most of the abovementioned terrorist actions were carried out by radical religious terrorist organizations from the Middle East is evidence of the situation.

2. Anticonventional terrorism: In this period, some terrorist actions, such as hijackings, bombings, and assassinations, were replaced by more complicated chemical and biological terrorism (bioterrorism) factors. One of the first examples this was when 750 people were poisoned at a restaurant in a town in Oregon, in the United States, in 1984. It was discovered that a terrorist organization that was operating in the region was responsible for the action. Members of the organization infected the salad bars in four area restaurants with the Salmonella bacteria (Zülal, 44).

The first examples of effective use of arms that cause mass massacre were seen in the 1990s; two tons of TNT was used just in the Oklahoma bombing (Övet, www.icisleri.gov.tr/id/dergi/446_189_214.doc).

In 1995, an attack in a Tokyo subway using a chemical agent called "sarin" signaled global terrorism. Twelve people died and 5500 people were injured in the terrorist attack, which was carried out by Aum Shinrikyo (or "Supreme Truth").

One of the major terrorist actions of this period occurred on April 19, 1995. Timothy McVeigh, a former soldier who had fought in the Gulf War, carried out a bomb attack on the Oklahoma City Capital building. McVeigh exploded the bomb, made of 2,200 kilograms of ammonium nitrate, in front of the building, killing 168 people. Timothy McVeigh was apprehended and later executed.

Currently, two factors relate to terrorist actions against tourism: extreme religious motives and bomb actions. The basis of these two factors was formed in the second period.

One of the main examples of religious terrorism and bomb actions targeted at tourism was the bombing of a hotel in Yemen on December 29, 1992, which American soldiers were using as a camp. It is striking that this was the first anti-American action that was connected to Bin Laden.

In this period, the most significant religious terrorist action occurred in November 1997 in Luxor, Egypt. In the attack, for which al-Gama'a al-Islamiya (Islamic terrorist organization) claimed responsibility; fifty-eight tourists were killed, including thirty-six Swedish, three English, and nineteen Japanese tourists. The Egyptians had to take precautions in order to increase the number of tourists, which decreased after the terrorist action.

Third Period: The air attacks on September 11, 2001, on the twin towers of the World Trade Center in New York City can be seen as the apex of the terrorist actions targeted at tourism that started in the second period.

September 11, 2001, saw the greatest terrorist action ever recorded, terrifying the Americans and the world. More than 3,000 American citizens lost their lives in the attacks on the towers of the World Trade Center in New York City, the Pentagon in Washington D.C., and on a plane that crashed in a Pennsylvania field. Noncombatant planes were exploited as mass-destruction weapons in those air attacks.

The timeline of the attacks, which had wide repercussions around the world, is as follows:

08:45 AM: American Airlines Flight 11 was hijacked with its eighty-one passengers and eleven crew members and crashed into the north tower of the World Trade Center in New York. No one realized at that time that the crash was a terrorist attack.

09:03 AM: United Airlines Flight 175 was hijacked with its fifty-six passengers and nine crew members and crashed into the south tower of the World Trade Center, as millions of people watched.

09:45 AM: American Airlines Flight 77 was hijacked with its fifty-eight passengers and six crew members and crashed into the Pentagon, the U.S. Ministry of Defense, which had been known as the best-protected building ever built.

10:10 AM: United Airlines Flight 93 was hijacked with its thirty-seven passengers and seven crew members, presumably headed toward the White House in Washington, D.C. Flight 93, however, crashed in Somerset County, Pennsylvania, as a result of the resistance of the passengers. All U.S. airports subsequently were closed to arrivals and departures, and planes that would use an American airfield were directed to Canada. The U.S. government announced a "red alert," a state of emergency, for the entire country.

The main impact of these attacks on the world economy is as follows:

- Most sectors in many countries in Europe suffered from the September 11 attacks. In September 2003 there was a decrease in the

rate of fullness of the hotels by 22.5 percent compared to the year 2000. That decrease was 38.4 percent in Paris and 21.9 percent in Rome.
(www.ilo.org/public/french/dialogues/sector/techmeet/imhcto1/update.pdf)

- The civil aviation sector is influenced by wars and terrorist acts. An example of this relates to the U.S. military operation against Iraq. Civil aviation traffic decreased by 10 to 15 percent, even at the beginning of the Iraq crisis, and this situation had a negative influence on the world finance sector (Girvan, 3).

- The civil aviation sector had a great loss after the September 11 attacks. The number of foreign visitors decreased by 12 percent in Australia, 2.1 percent in Hong Kong and visitors going to Europe, Africa and the Middle East countries after the September 11 attacks decreased by 2.7 percent. (www.ilo.org/public/french/dialogues/sector/techmeet/imhcto1/update.pdf)

- Approximately 4 million people are employed in the air transportation sector. Each plane is a direct job opportunity for 150 to 200 people, and 200 people might indirectly benefit from the opportunity. According to the International Air Transport Association (IATA), American air transportation lost $7 billion on international flights and $3 to $5 billion on domestic flights (Beaulieu & Essenberg, 4).

- September 11, 2001, was the time that the accommodation sector went through a severe bottleneck since 1938. In addition to that, the profit of the hotels decreased by 20 percent.

- Travel traffic decreased by 50 percent between Europe and America directly after the September 11 attacks.

- Bankruptcy rates in the Japanese accommodation sector increased by 20 percent, as compared to the previous year (2000) because of the September 11 attacks and the Japanese economic crisis.

- Directly after the September 11 attacks, the Australian Hotels Association (AHA) announced that there had been attempts to freeze the wages of the personnel who work in four- and five-star hotels for a period of six months.

- The research conducted by the World Travel & Tourism Council posited that ten million people had been influenced by the crisis after the September 11 attacks and many people had lost their jobs. The same research pointed out that world tourism regressed by 7.4 percent because of the September 11 attacks and America's shrinking economy.

- The September 11 attacks also influenced cruise tourism negatively; the tourist loss in the Kuşadası-İstanbul destination was between 750,000 and 800,000 people. Some luxury cruises, like Costa Atlantica, canceled voyages to Turkey.

- As a consequence of the September 11 attacks, Turkey lost 1.5 million tourists and $1 billion of tourism income in 2001.

- As a consequence of the September 11 attacks, travel insurance companies suffered a great loss, although insurance premiums increased in 2001. They stated that their balance sheet remained the same, as the number of accidents that required payment was more than 50,000 in 2001.

- The European Union authorized governments to aid airline companies whose safety and insurance outcomes dramatically increased.

Table 5: International Profile After the September 11 Attacks [*]

Air Traffic	8–28 October 2001 (%)	29 Oct.-18 Nov. 2001 (%)
In-Europe Flights	-14.6	-10.9
North Atlantic Flights	-33.0	-30.0
Far Eastern and Pacific Flights	-23.0	-18.8

[*]   (www.ilo.org/public/french/dialogue/sector/techmeet/imcht01/update3.pdf)

As it is seen in Table 5 (above), there was a decrease in number of intercontinental flights, as compared to the same period of the previous year.

Table 6: Rates (%) of Change in Post-September 11 Period Air Traffic in Comparison with 2000 [*]

Domestic Flights in the USA	-7/-13
Transatlantic Flights	-6/-12
Transpacific Flights	-4/+0
In-Europe Flights	-1/-5
Total International Flights	-6

[*] **Resource:** Bureau International Du Travail, Geneva, October 2001

As it is seen in Table 6, the decrease mostly was seen in domestic flights in the United States. While decrease in transatlantic flights was second to domestic flights, transpacific, and in-Europe flights suffered the least effects.

Table 7 shows that air traffic in all of the airports decreased after September 11, and O'Hare and Los Angeles Airports suffered the effects of terror the most.

Table 7: Increase and Decrease in the Number of Connected Passengers in the Busiest Airports in Post-September 11 (2001) [*]

Airport	Increase/Decrease (%)	Number of Passengers (Million)
Haneda	+3.5	5.18
Heathrow	-13.1	5.1
Frankfurt	-7.2	4.4
Hartsfield	-30.1	4.1
C. De Gaulle	-9.0	4.1
O'Hare	-34.1	3.9
Amsterdam	-5.1	3.6
Los Angeles	-33.1	3.5
Gatwick	-1.5	3.2
Madrid	-1.5	3.1

[*] **Resource:** ACI (Airports Council International) data

The bottleneck that American airports suffered after September 11, however, negatively influenced other airline companies all over the world. Rapid decrease in the number of flights and decreased demand caused a crisis in the aviation sector, mainly in America. AMR, which is affiliated with the world's biggest airline company Amirican, for example, lost 237 million dollars (www.havais.org.tr/metinler/brifing_20.doc).

Civil airline companies suffered a loss of $18 billion after September 11th, comprised of $12 billion in domestic flights and $6 billion in foreign flights. The Iraq War and SARS disease also influenced the civil aviation sector; the sector suffered a total loss of more than $30 billion at the end of 2003. 200,000 airport employers lost their jobs, and because unemployment in the aviation sector influenced other sectors, the total unemployment figure was 400,000 people (IATA, 2002).

In September 2001, while the passenger traffic of North American airline companies decreased by 33 percent, it dropped by 25 percent in the Far East, and Central and South America (Beaulieu & Essenberg, 4).

After the attacks, shares of airline companies in the stock market decreased seriously, in parallel with the decrease in the reliability of the airline companies. While the increase in the cost of insurance premiums dragged the airline companies into a bottleneck, increased security measures at the airports and on the planes meant additional costs for the companies.

The companies in Europe and Asia suffered serious loss because of the September 11 attacks. Swissair, one of the biggest airline companies in Europe, canceled its flights and declared bankruptcy. Sabena, a Belgian airline company, of which Swissair owns 50 percent of the stock, canceled its flights for an indefinite period of time. Air Libérté, the biggest airline company in France, Tab in Portugal, and Olympic Airlines in Greece also canceled their flights.

United Airlines, the second largest airline company in America and the world, declared a concordat because of its serious financial losses. Ultimately, twenty-eight airline companies declared a concordat or bankruptcy (Cebeci, 11).

Other negative effects on the civil aviation sector from the September 11 attacks are:

- In the days following September 11, AeroMexico and Mexicana Airlines suffered a loss of $6 million; Air Jamaique lost $11 million (Girvan, 3)

- Half of the business passengers and 60 percent of passengers with one-year leave canceled their flights (Girvan, 3).

- European and Asian airline companies were more fortunate than American companies in 2002. The financial loss was less in Europe and Asia because the number of passengers did not decrease as much as it did in America. Thai Airways, Malaysia Airlines, and the Philippines Airlines were indebted to their own states with more than 2 billion dollars, and TransBrazil laid off more than two thousand of its employees within three months (Beaulieu & Essenberg, 5).

- Air traffic in the world decreased by one-third, and the airline companies such as Alitalia, British Airways, and Swissair, which generally fly overseas, suffered most.

The World Tourism Organization stated that the number of the travelers, which was 697 million in 2000, decreased to 689 million in 2001, as a consequence of the September 11 attacks.

The profile of the tourist arrivals to the main destinations after September 11, 2001, is as follows:

Table 8: International Flights After the September 11 Attacks *

	2000	2001	2002
World	696.1	692.9	714.6
Europe	402.8	401.4	411.1
Asia-Pacific	115.5	121.0	130.6

Table 8: International Flights After the September 11 Attacks (Continued)[*]

	2000	*2001*	*2002*
America	128.5	121.0	120.2
Africa	27.0	27.7	28.7
Middle East	22.7	21.8	24.1

[*]   (www.ilo.org/public/french/dialogue/sector/techmeet/imcht01/update3.pdf)

The reflections of the September 11 attacks on international tourist arrivals in terms of subregions are displayed in Table 8, below. As is seen in the table, a decrease of 1.3 percent occurred in the world as a consequence of the terrorist actions. The sharpest decrease was seen in the Middle East, which is the source of the terrorism, and in America, which was the target of the terrorism.

Global terrorism, which took place in the world arena after September 11, 2001, has carried out terrorist events around the world, directly or indirectly targeting tourism. These are listed as follows:

- **August 9, 2001**: In a suicide attack occurring at a pizzeria in Jerusalem, fifteen people were killed and ninety were wounded.

- On **August 10, 2001**, the National Union for Total Independence of Angola (UNITA), which fights for the liberation of Angola in Cuanza-Norte, organized an attack on a train, killing 260 people.

- On **October 12, 2002**, explosions in nightclubs and restaurants on the Indonesian island of Bali, populated mainly by foreigners, killed 202 people and injured 132. The incident, known as the worst terrorist act ever recorded in Indonesia, and which directly targeted tourism, tourists from America, England, Germany, Japan, Belgium, Australia, and Sweden were among the dead and injured. The terror organization Al-Qaeda was responsible for the attack.

Table 9: International Tourist Arrivals on a Regional and Subregional Basis *

	January/August 2001 (Ratio to the same period of the previous year) (%)	September/December 2001 (Ratio to the same period of the previous year) (%)	Total
World	2.8	-10.9	-1.3
Africa	6.1	-3.5	3.2
America	0.3	-24.0	-7.0
North America	-0.1	-27.0	-8.2
The Caribbean	2.0	-16.4	-3.5
Central America	8.8	-10.5	3.0
South America	-2.2	-18.4	-7.1
Eastern Asia/	9.9	-10.3	3.8
Pacific	7.3	-8.7	2.5
Northeast Asia	15.3	-11.9	7.1
Southeast Asia	6.5	-15.2	0.0
Oceania			
Europe	1.7	-6.2	-0.7
Northern Europe	-3.8	-5.8	-4.4
Western Europe	2.3	-7.8	-0.7
Central and Eastern	2.8	-10.6	-1.2
Europe	1.5	-0.6	0.9
South Europe	7.3	-16.7	0.1
Eastern Mediterra-nean Europe			
Middle East	0.3	-30.2	-8.8
Southern Asia	1.2	-24.0	-6.4

*   **Resource:** (Le Tourisme Mondial En Perte De Vitesse En 2001), www.world-tourism.org, 03.08.2002

- On **November 28, 2002**, a suicide car bomb attack was perpetrated on a hotel, frequented mainly by Israeli tourists, in Mombasa, the major seaport in Kenya. Fifteen people were killed in the attack.

- In **November 2002**, a missile was fired from the ground at an Arkia Israeli Airlines Boeing 757–300, shortly after take off from Mombassa, Kenya, the first time such an incident took place as part of a terrorist attack on aircraft. Fortunately, the missile missed the aircraft.

- On **April 11, 2003**, Al-Qaeda bombed the historic synagogue on the Tunisian island of Dierba with a fuel truck. In the incident, fourteen German, one French, and four Tunisian people died.

- On **May 16, 2003**, an old Jewish cemetery and a luxury hotel preferred by Israelis in the center of Casablanca were targeted. The Belgian Consulate also was heavily damaged in simultaneous bomb attacks perpetrated on a Jewish-Italian-owned restaurant. More than forty people died in the five nearly simultaneous bomb attacks, occurring within thirty minutes and carried out by a team of thirteen suicide bombers.

- An explosion occurred outside a hotel in Jakarta on **August 5, 2003**. In the explosion of a car bomb parked in front of a Marriott Hotel, thirteen people died, 149 were injured, and there was a serious damage to the hotel lobby and nearby buildings.

- On **March 4, 2004**, a Nile cruiser caught on fire while on the water. A German passenger died and many tourists were injured.

- On **March 11, 2004**, during the train bombings carried out at three train stations in Madrid, the capital of Spain, 199 people died and thousands were wounded. It was claimed that the perpetrators were Moroccan and Algerian terrorists, who were members of the Moroccan Islamic Combatant Group.

- On **July 7, 2005**, during the five bomb attacks (three on the London underground and two on a double-decker bus), fifty-six people died and about 700 were injured. The blast blew off the roof of the bus. After the attacks, people were advised to stay in their homes. Even theater productions in the West End were canceled.

- After the blasts in London, the capital of England, on **July 7, 2005**, another four simultaneous bombings (three at subway stations and one on a bus) occurred in London.

- On **July 23, 2005**, suicide bomb attacks were perpetrated on two spots in Egypt's Red Sea holiday resort of Sharm al-Sheik. In the attacks, which were committed by the Abdullah Azzam Brigades, the Middle Eastern and Egyptian group of Al-Qaeda, a series of car bombs exploded in the driveway of the Ghazala Gardens Hotel in Naama Bay and the Old Market area. A few minutes after these explosions, a suitcase bomb exploded in a parking lot in Naama Bay. Then the fourth bomb exploded at the Movenpick Hotel near the Hazala Gardens Hotel. In these blasts, eighty-eight people died, including Turkish, English, American, and Czech tourists, and more than 200 were injured. After the blasts, the streets and beaches were emptied in the city, where the police tightened security and most people could not leave their hotel rooms.

- Almost three years after the first terrorist act on the Indonesian island of Bali, which is regarded as a holiday paradise, three simultaneous bombs exploded on **October 1, 2005**. Twenty-six people were killed, including Japanese and Australian tourists, and 101 were injured. While two of the bombings occurred in the seafood restaurant frequented by the tourists in Jimbaran, the third blast took place in Raja's Restaurant in Kuta, thirty kilometers away from Jimbaran. Susilo Bambang Yudhoyono, the president of Indonesia, condemned the blasts as "a terrorist act." It was suggested that the attacks were committed by Al-Qaeda.

Terrorist activities have had negative repercussions on travel, both directly and indirectly.

The security of the area to be visited often determines travel preferences. Of the 28 million Americans traveling internationally in 1985, 162 were killed during terrorist attacks (Kerourio, www.geotourweb.com/ nouvellepage12.htm). Many countries warn their citizens not to travel to the countries with high risk of terrorism.

For example, iJET Travel Risk Management rated 182 countries in terms of security risk and determined ten countries under risk of terrorism in its 2004 report. While Iraq, Afghanistan, and Somali were left out of evaluation, Spain, one of the most significant tourism destinations, took place among the ten countries with a security risk.

Colombia: FARC, Revolutionary Armed Forces of Colombia, perpetrated attacks targeting politicians and journalists, mainly in the rural areas. Moreover, the fact that at least eight people were taken hostage on September 13 in northern Colombia indicates that FARC intends to spread its terrorist actions for impact and results.

Indonesia: Indonesia has become one of the risky regions as a result of the bomb attack at the Marriott Hotel on August 5, 2003, in Jakarta. The government could not get the radical militants under control; thus, the anxiety of a possible attack to Western businesses emerged.

Israel: Terrorist actions and suicide attacks by Palestinian terrorist groups, particularly Hamas, targeting Israel can be considered a serious risk factor.

Russia: Terrorism threats, particularly in southeast Russia, have directly affected Moscow, which is a major tourism center. It was claimed that terrorist actions and sabotages targeting civilians might happen before the general elections in the country.

Spain: The ETA is reason that Spain, which is a significant destination in the world market, is one of the ten risky regions in the world. The organization aims to harm the country by targeting the Spanish tourism sector.

During the last thirty-five years, 800 people were killed because of the attacks carried out by ETA, whose main targets are police, hotels, and political party headquarters.

Thailand: An increasing number of terrorist attacks in the country make Thailand one of the risky regions. The location of the main tourist destinations and foreign businesses enables terrorist organizations to perpetrate hit-and-run operations; thus, terrorist actions have become easy. Authorities frequently warned the Thai government of a possible attack aiming at the Asia-Pacific Economic Cooperation Summit that was held in October 2004.

Moreover, it was declared in the iJET report that Kenya, Yemen, the Philippines, and Nigeria also are unsafe for international travel.

Reservations are canceled and destinations are changed when a country is declared to be unsafe for travel, either by the Ministries of Foreign Affairs or international institutions. For instance, North Americans changed their destination preferences and took short-distance flights after September 11 (Mowforth, 28).

Even though high-risk countries are pinpointed from time to time, it is very difficult to predict the target countries, as global terrorist organizations possess major technology and information systems. Therefore, terrorist actions targeted at tourism regions and tourists occur frequently, in spite of the warnings and precautions.

In 2001 local terrorist actions against tourism also occurred. The ETA, which aims to tarnish Spain's image and damage the national economy, generally organizing attacks on tourism businesses, carried out a series of actions against tourism in Spain.

The most extensive was four explosions that occurred on three trains on March 11, 2004, in Madrid. Eduardo Zaplana, a government spokesman, stated that the ETA was responsible for the actions. The explosions killed 191 people and injured nearly 400.

Apart from these unpleasant acts against tourism, the IRA, which is known for its tourism-oriented acts, declared an end to its armed struggle on July 28, 2005, thirty-five years after its founding, and stated that it would try to meet its aims through political means. The IRA has carried out acts with the aim of weakening the British economy and has targeted British tourists in Northern Ireland since the mid-1980s. The organization ended its terrorist acts after this declaration.

When the acts of the IRA are scrutinized, it is observed that it often targeted tourism, not tourists, as the main goal is to cause economic harm to a country through tourism. For instance, in a Heathrow Airport attack in

1994, after the IRA placed the bomb, they called the police and warned them to take precautions at the airport in order to prevent harm. (www.angelfire.com./folk/sosyolojik); (www.yesil.org./teror/irapkk.htm).

2.6. Terrorist Acts Targeted at Tourism in Turkey

Its geopolitical position, natural resources, and cultural richness brought about by social variety render Turkey superior in terms of tourism. These superiorities can form an available chaotic environment for countries that have different expectations of Turkey. Turkey provides an available setting for tourism but also for terrorism.

According to Dr. Emre Kongar, professor of sociology, Turkey has faced four tides of terrorism and is now about to face the fifth and final one. He explains the five tides of terrorism as follows (www.kongar.org):

1. The Armenian terrorism, which was international and aimed at representatives of the Turkish Republic. The Armenian terrorism ended when it struck France.

2. The left-right terror, between 1970 and 1980, was a war between the leftist terrorists, who wanted to seize the government, and the rightist terrorists, who already were inside the government but wanted to emphasize their sovereignty and take the democratic regime under their control.

3. The ethnic and separatist terror started in the 1980s and was referred to as "PKK" terrorism.

4. Radical Islamist terror started in the 1990s.

5. Inner subcontractors (domestic collaborators) who were protected and grew up at the end of this period came under the umbrella of global terrorism.

Many reasons lie behind the curtain of terrorist acts in Turkey, but they can be summed up in two ways:

- The expectations and strategies of some states and organizations toward the Turkish Republic, whose historical origin dates from Ottoman Empire
- The uneasiness felt by adversaries in return for the policies of the Turkish government with regard to international events

These factors helped terrorist organizations to survive, act, and thus, became a burden to the state budget in Turkey. Two factors influence the above mentioned for terrorism:

1. The ethnic richness of the population in Turkey
2. The geopolitical and geostrategical position of Turkey

The demographical and geographical structure of Turkey, especially, form a suitable ground for international terror, which allows terrorist acts to edge toward diplomatic and commercial targets in Turkey. Among the commercial targets, terrorist acts strike with the most efficiency at tourism, especially since the 1990s.

Two main elements are clear in the terrorist actions that directly target tourism in Turkey: acts of the Kurdistan Workers Party (PKK), which aim at the unitary structure of the Turkish Republic; and terrorist acts that do not necessarily aim at Turkish Republic but at the tourists visiting Turkey. Among this second group, actions against Russian tourists visiting Turkey (thus, Russian politics toward Chechenians) come first.

Even when they are not aimed directly at tourism, all terrorist acts have serious repercussions on tourism. For this reason, the events that aim at tourism as a priority will be dealt with in this section, followed by the major terrorist events with repercussions on tourism.

Terrorist organizations that are active in Turkey fall under three main groups, according to official data (www.sakarya.pol.tr/sizler/teror.asp):

- Marxist-Leninist terrorist organizations: DHKP-C etc.
- Separatist-racist terrorist organizations: PKK etc.

- Islamic terrorist organizations: Hizbullah etc.

- Foreign terrorist organizations: ASALA etc.

Among these terrorist organizations, only the PKK performs its operations directly against tourism at times. Although the other organizations do not aim at tourism directly, their operations indirectly have negative repercussions on tourism.

Bombing in the center of Antalya at the beginning of the 1993 tourism season was the first terrorist act against tourism in Turkey. Abdullah Öcalan, head of the PKK, announced that the PKK would attack touristic regions; this was followed by the first attack in Antalya on June 27, 1993. There were no casualties or deaths. On July 17, 1993, three hotels were bombed in a populated region in Antalya.

A year after the July 1993 attack, terrorist act against Turkish tourism shifted to Istanbul. The PKK executed a bomb attack in Kapalıçarşı-Istanbul on March 24, 1994, injuring four tourists, two of whom were women. Three days later the PKK executed a bomb attack in the yard of the Hagia Sophia Mosque. Three tourists—one Dutch, one German, and one Spanish—were injured.

On April 2, 1994, PKK carried out a bomb attack in Misir Bazaar in Istanbul. Two tourists—one from Belgium, the other from Spain—were killed and seventeen people were injured. On June 22, 1994, two bomb attacks occurred at two spots in Marmaris, one of which was a beach. One person was killed; eleven people, including four English tourists, were injured.

PKK militants carried out another bomb attack against tourism at the bus terminal in İstanbul-Topkapi. One Romanian consulate worker was killed and seven people were injured.

On July 13, 1995, PKK militants kidnapped a Japanese tourist on a road in Siirt; the tourist was released the next day.

On April 10, 1998, the PKK organized a bomb attack in a park near Blue Mosque in Istanbul. Seven people were injured; two were Indian tourists, and one was a New Zealand tourist.

On August 10, 2004, two bombs exploded simultaneously at the Holiday Hotel in Sultanahmet and Hotel Pars in Laleli. Two people were killed and eleven people, including several tourists, were injured. The attack was believed to have been organized by the PKK/Kontra-Gel militants.

Other terrorist actions occurred, the primary intension of which was to send a message to the Turkish government with regard to its foreign policy:

On November 15, 2003, two bombs exploded simultaneously in front of Neve Shalom Synagogue and Beth Israel Synagogue in Istanbul. Twenty-seven people died and hundreds were injured.

Five days later, terrorist bombings occurred again in Istanbul. A car bomb exploded in front of the HSBC Bank headquarters in Levant, and another exploded at the British Consulate in Beyoğlu. Thirty people were killed—among them, Roger Short, the British Consulate-General—and 450 people were wounded. As a result of these attacks, of the Dow Jones 600 Index, which tracks Europe's 600 largest companies, dropped by 7 percent, and travel and insurance sectors suffered greatly? (www.byegm. gov.tr/YAYINLARIMIZ/DISBASIN/2003/11/21×11×0.3.htm).

Terrorist events in Istanbul definitely had a negative effect on tourism demand toward Turkey. On the day when that the synagogue attacks happened, seventy room reservations were canceled in the Marmara Hotel. After the second attack there were even more cancellations (Bir, www. hurriyet.com.tr/yazarlar/0,sid~9). Following the bomb attacks in Istanbul, the Juventus Football Club players informed the Union of European Football Associations that they did not want to play in Istanbul.

Five thousand Italian tourists canceled their journey to Turkey following the Istanbul attacks; Japanese travel agents canceled the tours to Turkey after the Ministry of Japanese Foreign Affairs issued a warning against traveling to Turkey (www.hurriyetim.com.tr/haber/0,).

Terrorist acts continued during 2004. It is not clear, however, whether they were aimed directly at tourism. For example, on June 23, 2004, a bomb in a parcel was left opposite the Ankara Hilton Hotel. Its explosion, fortunately, did not cause any casualties. On June 29, 2004, a bomb exploded near a Turkish Airlines aircraft at Istanbul Airport. Three janitors were injured in the event.

Terrorist organizations are not solely responsible for actions against tourism in Turkey; the people who want to set an international agenda also have organized attacks. Chechen militants carried out many of these attacks against Russian tourists.

On January 16, 1996, seven Turks of Chechen origin hijacked a ferry carrying 180 passengers and forty-five crew members as it sailed from Trabzon to Russia (Soçi). The activists declared that they would release their Russian hostages on the condition that their friends under arrest in Dagestan were freed.

On March 15, 2001, a Russian Tupolev aircraft was hijacked after taking off from Atatürk Airport in Istanbul. The Chechen hijackers forced the aircraft to land in Medine. The event ended twenty-three hours later, due to the intervention of a Saudian special forces team, but a Turkish passenger, a stewardess, and one of the hijackers died during the operation.

On April 22, 2001, thirteen people protesting the war between Russia and Chechnya took 150 guests at a Swiss hotel hostage. No one was injured.

On May 3, 2002, an attacker carrying a Kalashnikov assault rifle invaded Istanbul's Marmara Hotel and held thirteen people hostage for ninety minutes. No one was injured.

The above mentioned three events were staged to send a message to the international public by intentionally using tourism. The events occurred shortly after the start of the tourism season and on specific days with heavy tourist traffic.

Turkey is a high-risk country because of its location, which is close to countries that experience conflict, tension, invasions, and war—this fact definitely affects the demand for international travel to Turkey. For example, with the help of England, the United States' invasion of Iraq meant that it was possible that the Middle East terrorists could carry out terrorist acts in Turkey.

A February 2004 risk assessment of 182 countries placed Turkey on the list of "Ten Riskiest Countries." Other countries on the list are Indonesia, Israel, Kenya, Colombia, Pakistan, the Philippines, Russia, Saudi Arabia, and Yemen. Because Turkey is at high risk of terrorism, the Ministry of Foreign Affairs in certain countries, as well as certain travel agencies, warn citizens against traveling to Turkey.

The above mentioned list does not include countries such as Afghanistan, Iraq, and Somali, where touristic and business travels have decreased because of the intense conflicts.

2.7. Crisis Management for Terrorist Events in Tourism

Tourism is the primary sector influenced by the effects of a crisis, regardless of the type of crisis. There are three main reasons for this:

1. Tourism interacts with several other sectors.

2. Tourism, by its definition, involves people (tourists). Abraham Maslow's hierarchy of needs emphasizes that psychological and safety needs are first in importance. Frederick Herzberg, who conducted research on human motivation, argued that when these two motives are not satisfied, human behavior will be affected negatively (Goguelin, 121–122). Simply put, tourists want to travel to countries where they can feel safe.

3. The tourism sector has an international dimension; tourism necessarily will be affected by internal or global crises, directly or indirectly.

Francesco Frangialli, secretary-general of the World Tourism Organization (WTO), emphasized that global tourism went through a tough period after 2001 because of the September 11 events, terrorist attacks, epidemic diseases, and the Iraq War. The number of international tourists dropped by 6 percent, and the growth rate of the world tourism receded to 0.5–1.5 percent from its previous growth of 2–3 percent (www.world-tourism.org/francais/newsroom/Releases/more_releases/Juin2002/chiffres2001.htm).

The process of crisis management in tourism is of great importance to businesses and countries alike, in order to appease or abolish the repercussions of crises.

Scientific research indicates that tourists welcome risk, up to a certain point. When considered in all aspects, negative events do not influence customer behavior, as long as the events are within the scope of the related individual's tolerance threshold (Glaesser, 56).

As far as it is possible to foresee crises before they occur, measures should be taken on a micro (businesses) and macro (state) scale against the possible crisis scenarios.

2.7.1. Crisis Management in Tourism on a Business Scale

Crisis management in businesses is defined as the organization of a plan against active possibilities and events that stem from the aim to reduce events that affect usual activities or works of a business or that reduce the capital or public image and threaten public health and safety, and which emerge all of a sudden (Vergilier, 26–27).

Crisis management also may be considered as the sum of all efforts, ranging from the plan to reduce the harm of crisis to the lowest level, to the evaluation of crisis signals beforehand and the measures taken in order to get over the crisis with minimum loss (Can, 45).

Businesses should follow a three-step-management process comprised of a before-crisis, during-crisis and after-crisis period. As it is difficult to foresee terrorism, a business, regardless of its size, must exercise the before-crisis and during-crisis techniques of strategic management (Kuhn, 194).

A business can receive crisis signals from two sources before a terrorism crisis: safety units (official safety organizations) and the media.

It is especially difficult for businesses to receive crisis signals from safety units. Business managers should pay careful attention to national and international media institutions and listen to terrorism experts. Administrators often may receive preliminary signals through these channels that indicate when political activity in the world is ripe to create a terrorism atmosphere.

Business management should be able to do a sound market analysis when the before-crisis signals are perceived. For example, an accommodation business (hotels, hotel villages) should be able to edge toward alternative markets.

A business can exercise several strategic management techniques during a crisis. The following techniques are exercised most often in the accommodation business:

- **SWOT Analysis**: Strengths, Weaknesses, Opportunities, and Threats (SWOT) analysis is an assessment of the internal and external situation in a business. The business's position is determined relevant to its competition and the market opportunities and threats are determined. Management performs a SWOT analysis, detects the business's weaknesses and the rival company's strongest three qualities, and then takes the necessary measures, according to this information.

- **Vision/Mission Statements**: A vision statement is the written announcement of the goals and principles on which a business is founded. The mission/vision statements aim to create a team spirit in a business against crises.

- **Conference Calling:** This technique aims to create one mind.

The main crisis management implementation for tourism businesses against terrorist events can be suggested as follows:

Tourism businesses should take internal measures against terrorist attacks, with safety first among these measures. Tourism businesses must do their best to protect their physical space against possible terrorist events. They should consult with official and private security institutions, and if the business has a special security unit, that unit should be informed of terrorism and current proceedings.

Some of the main measures taken against terrorism in international chain hotels are as follows:

- Hotel windows are covered with safety film.
- Safety barriers are placed in front of hotel entrances.
- Hotels are surrounded by fences (microwave instead of wire fencing).
- The use of closed-circuit imaging and recording systems at hotels. The installation of various systems is aimed at checking the entrances to the building and free zone (An area at a port or city where goods may be received and held without the payment of duty.), authorizing the entrance and exit of these areas, keeping records on a timely basis, receiving retrospective reports, detecting the people who are in the building and the location of those in the building, and ensuring security in the circulation of customers in an area.
- The installation of a biometric (fingerprint and hand geometry) entrance/exit control system that works with a card into the free zone of the hotel.
- The use of systems to check personnel attendance.

- The use of keys only by authorized personnel.

- Many hotels now use turnstile systems that allow the passage of only a limited number of persons in an approved entrance or exit procedure.

- The setup of automatic vehicle control systems (vehicle identifiers, road barriers, vehicle traps, sliding doors, roadblocking units) against terrorist attacks with vehicle bombs.

- The use of surrounding security systems as precautions, such as transmitting perceived threat to the local or central check point, watching and recording the threat, archiving past alarm recordings in order to analyze suspicious cases.

- The use of control checkpoints.

- The hotel is equipped with bomb or metal detectors.

- The setup of fire alarm and extinguisher systems and checking them regularly.

- Installation of GSM blocking devices are used in order to prevent bombings controlled by mobile phones, listening done by mobile phones, interviews within the guests of accommodation areas (e.g., convention hall, building, campus).

Accommodation businesses that worked to increase their international tourism also increased their precautionary measures against terrorism, especially after the September 11 attacks. Some businesses warn their hotel personnel and customers against possible terrorist events by using descriptions like "yellow alarm," which signals a possible terrorist attack, "orange alarm" (high-risk of terrorist attack), and "red alarm," which indicates a terrorist attack in progress.

Measures taken by businesses for an orange alarm are as follows:

- Form a special security area around the building

- Check all vehicles that approach the building

- Guests and personnel must carry ID cards

- Take digital pictures of those entering or leaving the building

Because terrorism is hard to foresee, businesses should form a crisis committee specific to planning for the possibility of a terrorist attack.

A crisis committee in the hotel business often is composed of the following:

- CEO
- General manager
- Vice general manager
- Controller (proposes precautions against terrorism with the available budget of the hotel)
- Human resources manager
- Purchasing manager

Steps in crisis process can be explained as follows (Aytemiz S. et. al., 109):

- The emergence of the elements threatening strategic aim and targets
- The ability/failure to perceive first crisis signals by a business
- The ability/failure of a business to take crisis under control

Perceiving crisis signals is significant to safeguarding a business against terrorist events. What should not be overlooked is that when operating in the international market, tourism businesses, especially, should be well prepared against a possible terrorist event.

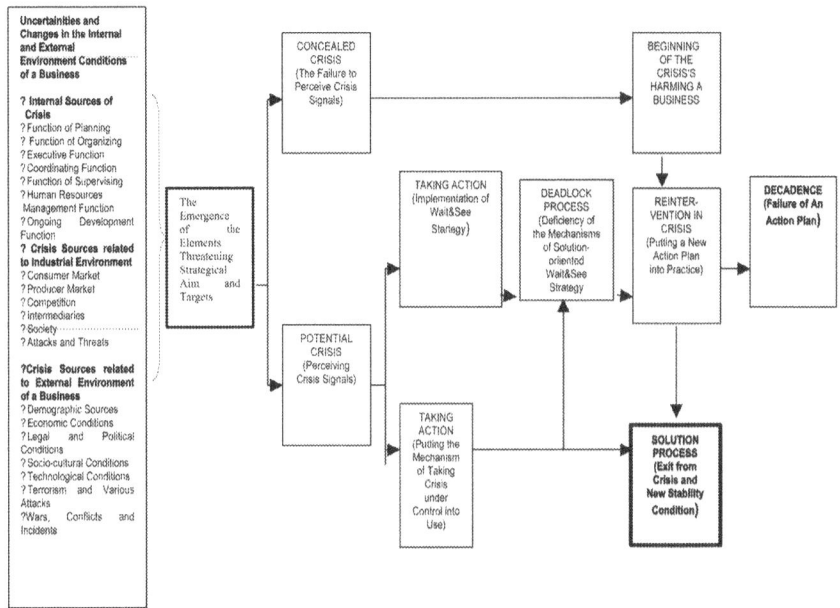

Figure 4: Crises, Their Effects, and Overcoming Crises in Tourism
Businesses: Crisis Management
Resource: AYTEMİZ, S.O.; BOLAT T. et al. (2004): "Turizm
İşletmelerinde Krizler, Etkileri ve Krizden Çıkış: Kriz Yönetimi,"
Verimlilik Dergisi, Ankara, MPM Yay.

The "intelligence phase" in a terror-oriented crisis management process involves the political tension in the world, warnings of either security forces or the leaders of terrorism organizations reported in the media. This stage can also be regarded as the threshold of perceiving crisis signals for tourism businesses.

This intelligence phase helps businesses to:

- Make rapid and right decisions
- Keep losses to a minimum
- Lower the tension and panic of employees and customers
- Increase the confidence felt toward the business
- Reduce costs during crisis

- Determine new opportunities through right strategies after crisis

The most obvious examples are the tapes made by Osama bin Laden, the leader of Al-Qaeda, which were broadcast on Al Jazeera TV in October 2003. Bin Laden stated that Al-Qaeda had the right to respond to all the countries who participated in the war, especially England, Spain, Australia, Holland, Japan, and Italy, at the proper time and place, pointing out the Iraq War. About five months after this statement, Madrid saw the most horrible attacks in its history. In the assault—ten explosions on four commuter trains—more than 190 people were killed and 120 people were wounded. Some businesses in Spain regarded the "moment of intelligence," which means a potential crisis, as October 18, 2003, the day bin Laden made a statement.

Because some businesses considered these statements to be the starting point of a crisis, they performed strategic analyses during the crisis period, and thus, the terrorism crisis caused little or no financial loss.

2.7.2. Crisis Management in Tourism on a National Scale

Terrorism reflects negatively both on businesses and the national economy. Tourism-oriented crisis management should be realized not only on a business scale but also on a national scale.

The intelligence phase, when terror signals are received, constitutes the starting point of the crisis management process, both on a national and business scale. Naturally, the most evident difference between business and national scales is that the state intelligence sources and the field are greater than in business. The breadth of the crisis area is a disadvantage, however, to the national crisis management process.

Regardless of the number of sources the state possesses, these should be at least a step ahead of the intelligence, financial, and technological opportunities of the terrorist organizations. This can be extremely difficult: states can be exposed to terrorist events like the September 11 attacks, which are considered a rare occurrence, but they can develop strategies against such attacks only after the events happen. Surely, tourism is among the sectors that suffer most from this process.

As in businesses, the crisis management process starts with the intelligence phase of terrorist events in a country. After terrorist signals are perceived by official channels, these signals should be evaluated rapidly, but done so without causing panic. Otherwise, the turmoil of the general public can trigger other crises. It is of great importance to educate people and raise their awareness before a crisis.

Today, the public is warned as soon as terror signals are perceived by state or national security units. For example, during the period that started with the U.S. invasion of Iraq, the U.S. Department of State raised the terrorist threat level from a code yellow to a code orange. In the United States, where it was suspected that Al-Qaeda might turn the holiday season into hell by using weapons of mass destruction, the code orange alert was in effect from December 24, 2003, to June 21, 2004.

After the September 11 attacks, the U.S. Department of State issued three regular warning notices for its citizens (http://travel.state.gov/travel_warnings.html):

- **Travel warnings:** These warnings are given to prevent Americans from traveling internationally.

- **Social warnings:** The warnings are given to signal a safety danger for Americans.

- **Embassy information paper:** These offer information (e.g., health conditions, drug punishments, customs formalities, etc.) on all countries.

Among the countries with a high risk of terrorism, Israel, like the United States, warns its citizens about traveling, according to terrorism-risk ratings. For example, Israeli security units warned its citizens not to travel to the south coast of Turkey on August 5, 2005, due to the high terrorism risk; it then warned them again August 8. Four Israeli passenger ships were directed away from Alanya to Cyprus, based on the available intelligence.

Two passenger ships carrying more than 1600 Israeli travelers were directed to Larnaca. The statement given by the Israeli prime minister's office warned all Israeli citizens not to travel to the area between Alanya and Kemer, Turkey. Israel's antiterrorism office also warned Israelis not to travel to the Sinai Peninsula in Egypt prior to the attacks in Sharm el-Sheikh in July 2005.

On August 12, 2005, the Israeli government removed the warning not to travel to Alanya and Kemer, after the arrest of a terrorist who confessed he had planned to bomb Israeli ships in Turkey.

Among the measures taken against terrorism in tourism, travel warnings for citizens should come first. Especially after September 11, people in America frequently are warned against potential terrorism with the color-coded alerts. In Europe, subway stations are closed for a certain period of time following any terrorism warning.

The general public lacks the knowledge of how to act against terrorism in Turkey. Intercorporate organization against terror, however, has improved.

During a violent act which resulted in death, injury, and physical damage in a touristic region, the Turkish Ministry of Tourism developed a crisis-management action plan, as follows (Turizmde Kriz Yönetimi, 12–16).

ACTION PLAN:

Incident: A violent act that results in the death or injury of tourists and physical damage in a touristic region.

The First Two Hours

Domestic Organization:

- Relevant provincial tourism administration bureaus shall inform provincial tourism administrators of the event.

- Relevant provincial tourism administrators shall inform the president or vice-president of the crisis-management team and soon after, they shall contact the civil service bureaus in the field of action, as well as local authorities of businesse s and/or tour operators welcoming the tourists.

Headquarters:

- After the Ministry is informed of the event, the members of the crisis management team (CMT) immediately shall be called for action.

- Relevant tourism information bureaus and provincial tourism administration bureaus shall be asked for detailed information.

- CMT shall contact the National Intelligence Bureau, Ministry of Internal Affairs, Ministry of Foreign Affairs, relevant governor's office and mayor's office, and central and local tourism bureaus.

- Foreign bureaus, especially those in the tourists' countries, shall be informed of the event and shall be ordered to follow foreign media; to what extent they can transfer information to others shall be determined.

Foreign Organization:

- Public relations agencies shall be informed; the portrayal of the event in media shall be watched, documented, and transmitted to general director of publicity.

- They shall contact the general consulate and/or embassy in the field of action and ensure coordination of the information that will be transferred to others.

The First Six Hours

Domestic Organization:

- Proceeding events shall be watched closely by the Provincial Tourism Administration Bureau and the Tourism Information Bureau and the information shall be gathered rapidly about those involved in the event, the tourists injured in the event—their identities, nationalities, their state of health, medical treatment, the relevant health centers, their contact information, tour operators—and constant information flow with the Crisis Management Team shall be ensured.

- Local diplomatic agencies (if available) shall be informed.

- Press relations shall be carried out coordinately with the CMT and the Department of Press and Public Relations.

- Relevant civilian authorities shall be warned to keep the press away from bloody images.

- The Ministry shall be asked for reinforcement personnel, when necessary.

- Relatives of the injured tourists shall be cared for.

Headquarters (CMT):

- The Crisis Management Team shall assess the information that they receive, determine the way to act and shall take action, making necessary adaptations in the before mentioned planned division of labor. Within this framework:

- Relevant foundations and institutions shall be informed of necessary directions, information, and requests.

- The information to be communicated by the spokesmen responsible for press relations shall be determined by the Department of Press and Public Relations.

- This information shall be formatted and reported to the authorized spokesmen (Department of Press and Public Relations, general director of publicity, undersecretary, minister at the headquarters, and relevant bureau representatives abroad).

- The information to be given to relevant diplomatic agencies shall be determined and reported.

- The portrayal of the event in domestic media shall be followed in a constant contact with the Department of Press and Public Relations and general director of Press and Information and assessed and when necessary overblown broadcasts shall be obstructed by the Department of Press and Public Relations. The portrayal in foreign media shall be watched through a constant information flow from foreign bureaus.

Foreign Organization:

- The portrayal of the event in foreign media and information demands arriving at the bureau shall be constantly reported to CMT.

- While the third party and institutions are informed of information, the borders determined by CMT shall not be crossed and action shall be taken in conformance with the directions of the PR agency.

- Necessary contact information shall be obtained from tour operators in order to contact the families of the injured tourists.

- The information sent from CMT shall be reported to the consulate general and/or the press consultancy.

The First 12 Hours

Domestic Organization:

- The health states of the victims of the crisis will be watched, their relatives at the place of the event shall be cared for, and the relevant information shall be reported to CMT.

- The contact with local tourism offices and civilian authorities shall continue. Any information, including arrest of the perpetrators of the event, the safety measures taken, and fixing of damages, shall be reported to CMT.

Headquarters (CMT):

- The portrayal of the event in domestic and foreign media shall be followed through the directorate general of Press and Information and Foreign Bureaus and assessed. The results shall be communicated to the consultancy of Press and Public Relations and general director of publicity.

- Whether there will be an official press statement or press conference shall be determined. If there is a press statement or conference, necessary organization and preparation of the statement shall be carried out with the collaboration of the consultancy of Press and Public Relations.

- The copies of press statements shall be sent to domestic and foreign organizations, the Ministry of Foreign Affairs, and relevant institutions of the sector.

- When necessary, meetings shall be held with sectoral institutions to exchange information, persuade them to confirm a decision, and determine the principles of cooperation.

- Messages shall be prepared for international tourism institutions, travel agencies, and media with the support of foreign PR companies via foreign bureaus. The copies of these messages shall be sent to domestic and foreign organizations, governor's offices and the Ministry of Foreign Affairs.

Foreign Organization:

- Official press releases for travel tips in market countries shall be closely watched, and if they contain statements that may affect the demand for the country negatively, the ministry shall be informed first, and necessary action shall be taken against this. In line with these initiations, the diplomatic agencies shall be convinced to take action and civilian pressure groups shall be formed with the collaboration of non-governmental groups, Turkey's friends, vocational tourism organizations, and tour operators marketing Turkey.

- The coordination and message unity shall be ensured between PR firms hired by diplomatic agencies for political publicity and lobby and the firms responsible for tourism PR.

- The information about the goings-on in the field of action shall be reported to CMT.

The First Twenty-four Hours and After:

Domestic Organization:

- The organizations shall continue caring for the victims of the crisis and communicating information about their state of health to CMT, to be reported to their families through foreign bureaus.

- Following victims' recovery, the organizations shall contribute to necessary organizations (by hosting, providing tickets, helping with departure) to help injured people and their families return to their countries.

- The occupancy rates and reservation trends of tourism businesses shall be watched, and the effects of the crisis on them shall be reported to the CMT.

Headquarters:

- Necessary information about changes in reservation trends shall be gathered from domestic organization and sectoral institutions and foreign tour operators through foreign bureaus and shall be assessed. The predictions on to what extent the crisis will affect meeting the expectations of estimated annual demand and income rate will be offered.

- When necessary, the general director of publicity shall order foreign bureaus to stop their advertising campaigns temporarily and design additional PR campaigns and send them to the headquarters, in order to focus on image repair.

- When necessary, revisions shall be done in foreign advertising campaigns about message, advertisement, media plan, and budget.

- The parts of the sector harmed by the crisis and the amount of loss shall be determined, and when necessary, additional programs that lessen the negative effects, increase competition forces, and revitalize the demand shall be developed.

Foreign Organization:

- The effects of the crisis shall be watched with all aspects, including reservation trends, level of consumer tension, portrayal in the media, counterattacks of competitors, and changes in market, and shall be reported to the Ministry.

- With the collaboration of advertising and/or PR agencies, the conformity of strategies of marketing communications, messages, creative techniques, advertisement sketches, and media plans shall be checked and, if necessary, revisions shall be done and presented to the director general of publicity.

Figure 5 shows the organizational chart of the Turkish Republic Ministry of Tourism against a terrorist event.

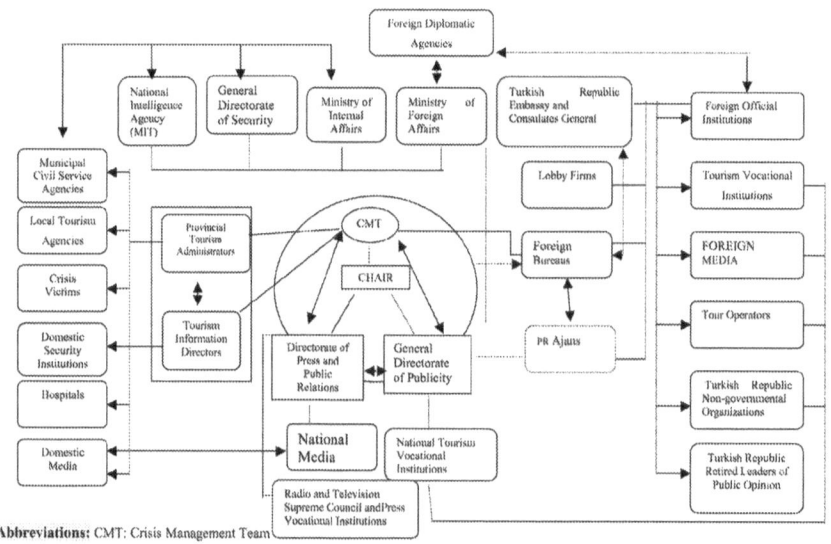

Figure 5: Turkish Ministry of Tourism Crisis Management Diagram

The increased risk of earthquakes has fortified the efforts of crisis management in natural disasters. The Marmara earthquake on August 17, 1999, and the Bolu and Düzce earthquakes on November 12, 1999, in Turkey revealed that the Turkish Republic governments, local governors, and nongovernmental organizations should be more organized in crisis management. As a result, several institutions formed crisis management desks. Public institutions, universities, nongovernmental organizations, and media also made positive efforts to educate society about earthquakes.

2.8. A Pilot Model on the Terrorist Actions Targeted at Tourism in Turkey

When travelers to Turkey are studied numerically, an upward trend is clear. While the number of travelers to Turkey was 13,256,028 in 2002, there were 14,029,558 visitors in 2004.

Four European countries were chosen for a pilot model on tourism-oriented terrorist events. The Germany, England, France, and Holland were analyzed in terms of their demand profiles.

Table 10: The Number and Rate of the Travelers Coming to Turkey from the Countries within the Study [*]

	2002	%	2003	%	2004	%
Germany	3,481,671	26.26	3,332,451	23.75	3,983,939	22.74
Holland	873,278	6.59	940,098	6.70	1,191,382	6.80
England	1,037,507	7.83	1,091,404	7.78	1,387,817	7.92
France	522,740	3.94	470,582	3.94	548,858	3.13

[*]   **Reference:** Data from Ministry of Culture and Tourism (04.22.2005): www.turizm.gov.tr

The total number of travelers coming from these pilot-model countries comprises, on average, 40 percent of all foreign visitors to Turkey (Table 9) The gradual decrease in Germany's ratio, which typically sends the majority of travelers, mostly stems from the existing economic problems in this country (an increase in unemployment, a decrease in real wages due to the currency conversion to the euro, etc.).

Table 11: Average Expenditure of the Travelers Coming to Turkey from the Countries within the Study (U.S. Dollars) [*]

	1993	*1995*	*1998*	*2000*	*2001*	*2002*
Germany	947	887	785	769	663	693
Holland	875	825	1089	975	845	664
England	912	804	899	814	749	690
France	868	829	810	796	613	710

[*]   **Reference:** Data from the Association of Turkish Travel Agencies (TURSAB) (04.22.2005): www.tursab.org.tr

The average expenditure of the tourists in Turkey, relevant to this study, has gradually decreased (Table 10); economic problems and global crises are among the top reasons for this. In addition, Turkey's inefficiency in terms of investment, marketing, and advertising policies for the selective type of tourists may be other factors (Kerr, 10).

2.8.1. Method And Model

In our study, a panel data analysis will be employed from a number of the methods for estimating tourism demand. In the analysis, time and cross-section series will be brought together, and a data set with both time and cross-section dimensions will be formed. Since the observations found in the cross-section are repeated over years, variance analysis models with repetition form the basis of panel data analysis (Pazarlıoğlu, 5).

Let us suppose that in panel data models, N denotes the number of economic units and T denotes the number of observations per unit. Here, the values that belong to a certain year denote the cross-section of a panel data set, while the values of economic units over years denote time. A time series corresponds to each economic unit. Therefore, considering two dimensions together comprises the panel data. The question, however, is how to define the econometric model that preserves the individual differences in the data collected with the aims of estimation and commentary.

It is possible to denote the panel data model as the following equation:

$$y_{it} = \beta_{1it} + \beta_{2it}x_{2it} + \beta_{3it}x_{3it} + e_{it}$$
$$i = 1,2,...N \ ; t = 1,2,...,T \tag{1}$$

In the general model above, the fixed regression parameter is allowed to vary for each individual in every time period. As this model contains many unknown parameters rather than data items, the structure of it cannot be controlled. Many simplifying assumptions can be made in order to enable the model to function. Ensuring accuracy is the definition of the econometric model that emerges from the data production process.

The Fixed-Effects Model and the Random-Effects Model, two of the simplified models of the econometric model mentioned in the equation no. 1, will be discussed in this section. It is assumed that in both models, errors of e_{it} are assumed to spread independently and in the form of $N\ (0,\sigma_e^2)$ for all individuals in every time period.

These models can be explained as follows:

2.8.1.1. Fixed-Effects Model

It is assumed in the general formulation of the fixed model that the differences between units can be met in the differences in fixed term. For this purpose, the panel data model is estimated through a dummy variable. When the model number one is considered, the following is assumed:

$$\beta_{1it} = \beta_{it} \qquad ; \beta_{2it} = \beta_2 \qquad ; \beta_{3it} = \beta_3 \tag{2}$$

Here, only the fixed parameter varies, and the fixed term varies not according to time but in terms of cross-section. When both the dimensions of time and cross-section are taken into consideration, the following model is obtained:

$$y_i = x_1 \, \beta_{1j} + X_N \, \beta_S + e \tag{3}$$

Model number three is generally connoted as Least Squares with Dummy Variable (LSDV). When the final equation is considered, it becomes apparent that there are different fixed effects for different individuals. *Is such treatment of the model appropriate? Or is a model where all parameters are assumed to be equal for the N number of individuals appropriate?* If all parameters are the same and other assumptions prove valid, there are no behavior differences among individuals and time dimensions. Thus, the data can be taken as an example of NT observations set. Here, as the intra-group differences matter, the hypothesis that fixed terms are equal can be probed by F test.

2.8.1.2. Random-Effects Model

The behavior differences observed in each individual with a different fixed parameter were explained above by means of a model with a dummy variable. Under this title, another model that is more useful is employed, when the example individuals are chosen randomly or an individual is taken from its main mass as a representative. Here, when individuals are chosen randomly, the individual differences (happening to an individual) observed are random too. The mentioned differences are called random effects. Random effects are the result of a sampling process. Therefore, in equation number one:

$$y_{it} = \beta_{1i} + \beta_{2it} x_{2it} + \beta_{3it} x_{3it} + e_{it}$$
$$i = 1,2,...N \; ; t = 1,2,...,T$$

β_{1i} is taken as a random variable and the following equation is obtained:

$$\beta_{1i} = \beta_1 + \mu_i$$

Similar to systematic transformation-based parameter models, when the parameter transformation model in equation number four is placed in model number three, the following is obtained:

$$y_{it} = (\beta_1 + \mu_i) + \beta_{2it}x_{2it} + \beta_{3it}x_{3it} + e_{it}$$
$$i = 1,2,...N \; ; t = 1,2,...,T$$

$$y_{it} = \beta_1 + \sum_{k=2}^{k} \beta_k x_{kit} + (e_{it} + \mu_i) \tag{5}$$

The expression in number five is the main form of the error component model. The expression "error component" stems from the term of $e_{it} + \mu_i$. This term is composed of two components: While e_{it} demonstrates all errors, μ_i shows "specific" error, individual differences, and the variation between individuals.

Since $w_{it} = e_{it} + \mu_i$, it is possible to write the model as follows:

$$y_{it} = \beta_{1i} + \beta_{2it}x_{2it} + \beta_{3it}x_{3it} + w_{it}$$
$$i = 1,2,...N \; ; t = 1,2,...,T \tag{6}$$

The Random-Effects Test: Lagrange Multiplier Test was developed for the random-effects model, based on OLS (Ordinary Least Squares) errors. The null hypothesis ($\sigma_\mu^2 = 0$), where random effects are null, are searched by this test.

The Hausman Test (Hausman Specification Test) is employed in order to test whether the distinct difference between fixed-effects or random-effects models is related to independent variables. When the random-effects model is valid, fixed-effects estimators still provide parameter estimations that can be estimated consistently. The fixed-effects estimator should not be preferred to the random-effects estimator, as long as one is not sure whether all the fixed-time factors related to other independent variables can be measured (Johnston, J & Dinardo, J., 403).

Many researchers find the act of estimating fixed effects more convincing than estimating random effects. This preference stems from the idea that it is not possible for fixed effects to be unrelated to relative explanatory variables except in full testing and half-testing cases.

Neither the fixed-effects estimator nor the random-effects estimator is perfect. While the random-effects estimator gives deviation estimations above the real effect, the fixed-effects estimator is also known to give deviation estimations below the real effect (Johnston, J & Dinardo, J., 405).

At this point, "*Which model should be used?*" becomes an inevitable question. So far, two estimators have been developed depending on the relationship between b_{1i} and explanatory variables. Especially:

- If effects are unrelated to explanatory variables, the random-effects estimator (RE) is consistent and active. The fixed-effects estimator (FE) is consistent but not active.

- If effects are related to explanatory variables, the fixed-effects estimator is consistent and active, but the random-effects estimator is inconsistent.

- The Hausman Test statistics demonstrates the chi-square distribution with a k-degree of freedom under the null hypothesis that the "random-effects estimator is accurate."

If the coefficients of explanatory variables do not show the best linear unbiased estimator and if fixed effects are random, it would be more appropriate to use the method of Generalized Least Squares (GLS).

2.8.2. Applications

In this study, the demand for tourism products and services is seen as a demand for any good or service. A crosswise data set of the aforementioned countries between 1992 and 2002 has been used, in order to identify tourism demand in Turkey. The focus is on yearly data in order to remove the seasonal effect. The elements that affect the demand for tourism products and services can be summed up as follows:

- Revenue of importing country
- Cost of goods and services of exporting country
- Exchange rates
- Population

There are many alternative ways of estimating tourism demand: the income from foreign tourists, the number of nights that foreign tourists spend in the country, and the number of tourists coming from every country. In this study, however, the number of tourists will be taken as a dependent variable. The fixed-dollar exchange rate of each country's GNP in 1995 is taken into consideration as an explanatory variable.

Moreover, the Gross National Product (GNP) of each country has been divided into that country's parities of purchasing power, in order to maintain homogeneity and to compare itself with other countries. These values have been divided by each country's population in order to obtain the GNP per capita.

Another explanatory variable is the price of tourism services in Turkey. The price index for culture and recreation prepared by the State Institute of Statistics (SIS) is regarded as a tourism price. This index was divided by the consumer price index of each country (CPI) and has turned into real terms.

The exchange rate of Turkish lira against the mentioned countries' national currency units, however, has been assumed as an exchange rate variable. Logarithms have been employed linearly to gain elasticity in the models in the following way:

$$LTUR_{it} = a_{it} + \beta_1 LGDP_{it} + \beta_2 LEX_{it} + \beta_3 LPR_{it} + U_{it}$$

Here, above, the subindices express "i" country, "t" time, and "L" logarithm.

$LTUR_{it}$ = the logarithm of the number of tourists coming to Turkey from the "i" country during "t" year.

β_i = the fixed term, which bears the complex characteristics of countries and which has been neglected.

LEX_{it} = the logarithm of the foreign exchange rate of "i" country equivalent to Turkish lira per unit during "t" year.

LPR_{it} = the logarithm of the price index of tourism services in Turkey, divided by each country's Consumer Price Index (CPI).

When the distribution of European tourists coming to Turkey in 2004 is studied according to their nationalities, it is seen that Germany, England, Holland, and France have a great share. Respectively, Germany has a share of 23 percent, England 7 percent, Holland 6.9 percent, and France 3 percent, in tourism demand. That constitutes 40 percent of total tourism demand.

In fact, the rate of tourists coming to Turkey from the Commonwealth of Independent States is 16 percent, but since the aim of the study is to evaluate the analysis of the tourism demand of Western European countries toward Turkey, the study has been restricted to these four countries only.

2.8.3 The Results of Application

In this study, a data set has been used that covers an eleven-year-period of four Western European countries that demand tourism service from Turkey. The model is advantageous, although it is a prediction, in order to diminish the degree of freedom that has been lost in the predictions using the compound of the time and cross-section data of these countries. The results, which were obtained through different methods of prediction, are shown below in Table 11. The predictions were obtained by means of Ewives software package

Some of the predicted models are shown in Table 11. The model in the first column of the table is a combined model that was predicted by the Least Squares Method. This model assumes that the demands of all countries do not change over time, there is no difference between the fixed values (i.e., average demands), and the gradient coefficients of the explanatory variables are the same for Germany, England, Holland, and France.

The assumptions for the model, which is predicted in the second column of the table, are within the Fixed-Effects Model that presumes there is variability among the average demands of the four countries, but which regards the gradient coefficients of these countries as fixed. In this model, there has been an attempt to specify that the differences between the variations in the demands of the countries may result from value judgments or the cultural structure of each country. Furthermore, this model emphasizes the fact that the variation in the demands of each country may result from the changes over time, although the average demand of each country is different.

Table 12: The Results of the Models That Were Obtained through Different Methods of Prediction *

Explanatory variable	(1) Common No Weighting (OLS)	(2) Fixed Effect Cross Section (GLS)	(3) Common Cross Section Weighting(GLS)	(4) Common No Weighting (OLS)	(5) Common Cross Section Weighting (GLS)
Fixed	-30,678 (-17,09)	Fr-25,25 Al-24,24 Uk-27,18 ND-24,5	-32,46 (-24,26)	-18,715 (-6,407)	-15,10 (-4,267)
$LGDP_{it}$	0,5627 (9,7287)	0,14747 (1,06)	0,573 (10,181)	0,391 (6,41)	0,2962 (4,197)
LPR_{it}	-0,2415 (-1,212)	-0,05029 (-0,25)	-0,339 (-2,235)	-0,258 (-1,451)	-0,203 (-1,715)
LEX_{it}	0,3105 (1,58)	0,2244 (1,036)	0,518 (3,530)	0,301 (1,76)	0,291 (2,289)

Table 12: The Results of the Models That Were Obtained through Different Methods of Prediction (Continued)[*]

Explanatory variable	(1) Common No Weighting (OLS)	(2) Fixed Effect Cross Section (GLS)	(3) Common Cross Section Weighting(GLS)	(4) Common No Weighting (OLS)	(5) Common Cross Section Weighting (GLS)
LTUR$_{ij}$(-1)				0,4485 (4,67)	0,567 (5,187)
$\bar{R}^2$	0,7524	0,997	0,994	0,84	0,998
F	44,56	7300,74	2504,3	52,49	5006,97
Se	0,81	0,608	0,736	0,679	0,635
D-W	0,991	1,32	1,226	1,629	1,931

[*]   Dependent Variable: LTUR$_{it}$

The difference in tourism services that are demanded from Turkey from all the countries in the world possibly can be estimated through the Error Components Model (ECM) and the Random-Effects Model (REM) to reveal the differences among these four countries, as well as others, where the services have been fixed. The estimations of these models are not shown in this table, as they have been found statistically insignificant. The reason this model is invalid is that the fixed value of each country results from the differences among countries (i.e., it results from the relation between the error components and the explanatory variables of those countries).

The error components of the countries can be examined as elements, such as the history, the culture of each country, and its background knowledge about Turkey. Therefore, the Fixed-Effect Model (FEM) may be more suitable than the Error Components Model (ECM). In Table 3, Generalized Least Squares (GLS) estimations have been used to obtain the best linear estimations in the first and second columns.

Primarily, when the indicators of all model parameters previously estimated are examined, whether or not they are according to economic expectations, they have been found out to be in harmony with economic expectations. Secondly, when the estimated parameters are analyzed in terms of statistical significance, all parameters are found significant in the first and third models, as the values in parentheses under the parameters give t statistics. Thirdly, an autocorrelation has been found in the first model as a result of the changing variance and autocorrelation tests, with respect to the assumptions of the error components. The parameters, however, have not been found statistically significant in the second model.

The model that supports the study is the third one estimated through Generalized Least Squares (GLS) Method. This model provides the best linear unbiased estimations (BLUE).

Thus, the flexibility of the income in tourism goods and services that are demanded of Turkey is +0.573 as a result of this practical study. This value verifies the hypothesis that the travel demand for the foreign tourists in Turkey is not luxurious.

In the same way, the flexibility of the prices is -0.339. The flexibility in the rate of the demand is 0.518; therefore, the price and the rate are not more flexible than the demand. The estimated flexibility for the exchange rate is +0.518; this is significant. This means that there will be an increase of 0.57 percent in the international flow of tourists to Turkey because of the percentage of increase in the Turkish lira per foreign exchange unit. The models that have been estimated so far are static models.

Dynamic models also were used in this study, because tourism supply has a different structure. Potential habits of a country and the desire of tourists to come to the same district again (due to quality of service and hospitality in that region) require that the delayed variables of the tourists be included in the model.

In the same way, it is possible to include the delayed values of price variables into a model. The models in the fourth and fifth columns in Table 3 have been estimated to this end. Dynamic models have not included these models, as price variable was found to be insignificant.

The best dynamic model, according to the model selection criteria, is the model in the fifth column. In the dynamic model, the indicators of the variable parameters are according to the economic expectations, and these parameters are significant as a result of the statistical and econometrical tests. Thus, an increase of 0.56 percent is shown in tourist demand after their travel to Turkey, for those living in Western Europe.

This study concludes that the most important factors that affect the demands of the four Western European countries for tourism products and services in Turkey are income, price, and exchange rates. When the estimation models have been considered, it is obvious that the model in the third column is the best among the static and dynamic models.

Flexibility of income, according to this model, has been estimated as +0.573, flexibility of price is -0.339, and flexibility of the exchange rates is +0.518 in the study. The results of the estimations of the dynamic models reveal that the model in the fifth column is best. Flexibility of the income, according to the dynamic model, has been estimated as +0.296, flexibility of the price is -0.203, and the flexibility of the exchange rate is +0.291. On the other hand, flexibility in the demand for the delay of the tourists coming to Turkey is +0.567.

All these results should be interpreted meticulously, as it is difficult to differentiate tourists' reasons for coming to Turkey in the data used.

2.9. Terrorism, Tourism, and Media Relations

One of the most important efforts of a crisis-management process is the communication of state with the media, during and after a crisis. Media, which is called "the fourth force" in democratic countries, increases its activity in world public opinion in parallel with the development of technology.

Even in the United States, which is considered a world superpower, media institutions play a large role in evaluating the public's response to important political decisions. For example, foreign policy specialists in Washington closely follow the media because they believe that public attitude with regard to foreign politics relates to global media (Nacos, 17).

Therefore, a terrorism event, which threatens civil life and uses media as a means, should be treated sensitively. Indeed, this is a valid suggestion not only for news of terrorism but for all news. Any news, when exaggerated by the media, can trigger a national crisis.

One of the most interesting examples in this context occurred in Greece. Greek media announced that a turkey was infected with a bird flu (avian influenza), noting that "Bird flu has broken out in Greece too." The panic-stricken Greek government put the island of Inusses under quarantine—until it became clear that the turkey was not infected.

Terrorists and the media often seem to have mutual expectations; that is, the media has expectations with regard to a terrorist (or act of terrorism), and terrorists have expectations of the media. These expectations sometimes overlap, creating a serious threat against travel and tourism.

The terrorist's expectations of the media, following to an act of terrorism, are as follows:

- A terrorist wants to communicate his/her act to the masses through the media.
- A terrorist wants to send a message.
- A terrorist wants to augment economic losses caused by his/her act through media.
- A terrorist releases fear and panic, which are his/her main aims, through media.

The media has two principal expectations of a terrorist event:

- To inform public opinion

- To present news in different aspects than other media institutions, which will increase sales

The most important task of media is to present news without exaggeration and unnecessary sensationalism. Commercial concerns bear importance, too, but in this context, there should be a careful balance between commercial concern and public responsibility.

The most important factor in a crisis-management process is the portrayal of the crisis in the media in the country in which it occurred. The international dimension of this portrayal is more important than its national dimension, because economic competition between countries enables competitors to turn terrorism to its own advantage and ensures that news will be more active on the agenda.

Terrorist events against tourism reflect on the media in three ways:

1. Agenda-setting (for commercial sales): Announcing news differently than other news institutions and increasing the ratings or sales

2. Preparing news in line with public responsibility (positive aim): Announcing news while keeping in mind that reservation cancellations in a country may have a negative effect on the country's economy

3. Providing support for terrorism (negative aim): Confining news to a quadrangle of corpse/blood/casualty/screams and decorating the news with hyperbole, dramatic background music, and excited voices.

Commercial news can have an encouraging effect on terrorists and helps terrorists' aims. For example, at his trial in January 1996, the leader of those who hijacked the Avrasya boat stated that they had planned to drop off Turkish passengers on the boat in Samsun. They changed their minds, however, when they saw on TV that there would be an operation against them.

Mass communication outlets must consider public interest, primarily about terrorism news, in their own rules. For this reason, a filtered-news method gradually has gained importance in Europe.

Filtered news is "the sum of the processes of reflecting crisis-focused news, filtered through media on public opinion, without any legal obligation, when necessary, for the interest of the country, and enlightening media employees in order to do that" (Küçükaltan, 52).

The United States was one of the first implementers of filtered news. During the bomb attacks in Oklahoma City in April 1995 and in Istanbul in November 2003, the approach of the media was as follows (www.aym.itu.edu.tr/terorist/12.pdf+Oklohama+city+sald):

CBS News, one of the biggest mass communication groups in the United States, laid down some rules for its personnel with regard to the announcement of terrorist events to the public (Alparslan, 74):

- The demands of terrorists shall be reported, not directly in their own words but in a press member's words.

- As a terrorist's words are communicated, his video shall be broadcast for a short time.

- Except in obligatory cases, live broadcasts shall be performed less often.

- Any display of a terrorist event shall not delay other news of the day.

- Even if press members know where a terrorist is, they will contact public officers and activists.

April 19, 1995/Oklahoma	November 15 and 20, 2003/İstanbul
Media had negative effects on the intervention at first. Inaccurate and speculative news was given. For example, while one TV channel told health personnel to go to the area, the other told them to go to the area and wait. Measures were taken in order to keep the media out of the area. The media was regularly provided with information. They gave only attested information that would not affect the inquiry. Press conferences were regularly held by the police, fire department, Ministry of Public Works, and FBI.	When events occurred for the first time, rumors about other explosions in Göztepe and some other places on the Asian side caused people to panic. Some members of the media went into the debris, risking their lives. The media was not provided with information on a regular basis. Press conferences were not held regularly. Because of that, members of the media had to receive information from other sources.

In a filtered-news model (FNM), the chance of seeing the crisis via the media is reduced, as the frequent news reports may lead to doubts about the deliberateness of news. For instance, the act of a Chechen activist in Istanbul at the Marmara Hotel on May 3, 2002, was portrayed to the public as an advertising spot that was repeated every half an hour on French TV.

In a filtered-news model, the language, vocabulary, and style in which terrorist events are shown is important, as it is assumed that the language used in news and commentaries reflects propaganda (Coward&Ellis, 32). For this reason, language should be chosen meticulously, in terms of semantics, during the treatment and introduction of terrorist events.

The language of the news can make people's fear increase, or it can lower social tension. *El Pais*, a newspaper published in Spain, reported the terrorist events of the ETA, which have become routine, by using the headline "Holiday Continues Despite ETA." The paper stated that the ETA routinely carries out bomb attacks along the coast during summer months, but none of these attacks would be able to affect Spain's record tourism (www.christusrex.org/wwwl/news/7-96/fm7-23-96.html). Such a style helped to attenuate the effects of terrorism.

According to Erkan Mumcu, the Minister of Culture and Tourism, since the media released exaggerated news about a fire at Mavi Çarşı shopping center, the world public opinion has been that Turkey is a country with a high security risk. This led to a $4-million loss of revenue, and 250,000 people lost their jobs (NTV Metinler, 04.24.2001).

The media clearly has a great impact on the general public; that is, public opinion tends to follow media commentaries on terrorists' motives and the essence of the situation (Kerourio, www.geotourweb.com/nouvellepage12.htm). Such situations can be alleviated by using a filtered-news model.

A filtered-news model basically has an implementation of two stages: *training* and *control*.

1. Media personnel must receive some training to employ a filtered-news model. This includes members of the national media, as well as local media.

2. During the control process, two systems emerge: *legal control* and *self-control*.

While states interfere with the news released by media in certain countries, some countries have less rigid legal arrangements. In Great Britain, the press is warned with the system called "Defense Notice System." This lets media representatives know that the release of certain news, primarily that of the IRA, may harm state security.

The governmental bodies in Turkey, at times, use censorship of the media after a crisis. For example, in 2000 the Turkish State Security Court, Chief Public Prosecutor's Office, stopped the news that protested F-type prisons, issuing a statement claiming that the media had presented superfluous news.

Most importantly, members of the media should be made aware of the fact that news can trigger crisis. Modern communication technology allows news of a terrorist event to spread throughout the world in a short time.

News of the synagogue and HSBC Bank bombings that occurred at ten o'clock in the morning in Istanbul was announced on a Web page at ten thirty. (www.lemonde.fr.web/article). While such expediency leads one country into a crisis, however, it enables other countries to take measures in order to turn the crisis into an advantage. The manner in which terrorist events are reflected in the media is important in terms of the accuracy of the news, as well as with regard to security.

Conflicting data on terrorist events released by the media can have a negative effect on tourism. For example, one Internet site announced that there were no deaths or casualties in the bombings after the PKK blasts in Antalya in 1993, whereas another site claimed that twelve tourists were among the "28 casualties in the attack at three hotels" (www.mediasnews.com/chrono/chrono1993php).

CONCLUSION

Tourism is growing rapidly in the world, and projections indicate that it will maintain its rapid growth in the twenty-first century. This growth in tourism has led to serious competition among the countries with tourism potential.

Many factors ensure tourism's development, and three phenomena constitute the basis of these factors: globalization, New World Order, and economic integrations (e.g., EU, NAFTA, and ASEAN). While all three phenomena have increased international travels, they also have increased the number of international businesses in an intensely competitive environment.

Globalization has increased touristic supply and demand, but it has globalized crises as well. Crisis environments in a particular country have been able to spread to other countries in the way a stone forms circles in still water. Epidemic disease, economic depression, and political crises that began in Georgia in early 2000 spread to neighboring countries in a domino effect. Global terrorism also spreads in this rapid fashion.

Globalization has not only led to internationalization in tourism but also in terrorism; international terrorism has focused on international tourism. Travel facilities have more travel restrictions because the travel formalities have been increased—tourism and tourist safety has become a primary concern in every country.

Ethnic separatism-based terrorism in a national context also chooses tourism as a target. As a result of this, the extent to which terror and tourism overlap is apparent.

The role of tourism on countries' macroeconomic indicators and the fact that tourists are the indefensible representatives of a target country render tourism attractive for terrorists. This is the reason that terrorist attacks have targeted the tourism businesses and the reason that many tourists have been victims of terrorism.

While tourism is the artery of terrorists, media is the oxygen for terrorism. It is responsibility of the media to reduce the effect of a terrorist action when reporting to the public and to prevent terrorists from reaching their goals. It would be a democratic approach for media institutions, which are supposed to walk the thin line between commercial and public responsibility, to go beyond this dilemma with self-control, rather than legal arrangements.

Look forward to seeing the dark side of terror illuminated with the peaceful light of tourism.

BIBLIOGRAPHY

BOOKS

ADİL, İ., and T. AKTAŞ. *Türkiye'nin Kayıpları ve Olası Riskler.* www.forumfuar.com, 2004.

AKAT, İ., and G. BUDAK. vd. *İşletme Yönetimi.* İzmir, Başarı Yay, 2002.

AKTAN, C.C. and I.Y. VURAL. *Globalleşme: Fırsat mı, Tehdit mi?* Istanbul, Zaman Kitabevi, 2004.

ALKAN, N. *Gençlik ve Terörizm*, Ankara, TEMUH Yay., No. 9. 2002.

ALPARSLAN, M.Ş. *Kriminoloji ve Hukuk Açısından Tedhişçilik*, Istanbul, Tenki Yay. 1983.

ALTUĞ, Y. *Terörün Anatomisi.* 1. Bsk., Istanbul, Altın Kitaplar Yay. 1995.

BAŞOL, K. *Türkiye Ekonomisi.*Eskişehir, AÜ Yay., No: 876. 1997.

BORET, A. *Itineraires de Tourisme*, Paris, Editions Jacques Lanore. 1989.

CAN, H. *Organizasyon ve Yönetim.* Ankara, Siyasal Kitabevi. 1997.

COWARD, R.; ELLIS, J. *Dil ve Maddecilik.* Çev:E.Tarım, İstanbul, İletişim Yay. 1999.

CROSS, J.C. *Tourism, Terrorism and Tyranny.* www.openair.org/cross/tour.html, 09.13.2004.

DALLI, Ö. *Turizm Talebi ve Gelirleri.* Ankara, Ajans-Türk Matbaacılık. 1974.

DİNÇER, Ö. *Stratejik Yönetim ve İşletme Politikası.* 5. Bsk., İstanbul, Beta Yay. 1998.

GLAESSER, D. *Turizm Sektöründe Kriz Yönetimi.* çev:A.B.Ahıska, İstanbul, Set-Systems. 2005.

GOGUELIN, P. *Le Management Pyschologique des Organisations.* Tome: 2, Paris, ESF. 1992.

HOFFMAN, B. *Inside Terrorism.* New York, NY: Columbia University Press. 1998.

İLHAN, S. *Terör: Neden Türkiye?* 2. Bsk., Ankara, ASAM Yay. 2002.

JOHNSTON, J. and J.DINARDO. *Econometric Methods,* 4 ed. New York, NY: McGraw-Hill. 1997.

KERR, H.D. *Educational Policy: Analysis, Structure and Justification.* D.McKay Company. 1976.

KONGAR, E. *Küresel Terör ve Türkiye.* 7. Basım, İstanbul, Remzi Kitabevi. 2003.

KUHN, R.L. *Creativity and Strategy in Mid-Sized Firms.* New Jersey: Prentice-Hall. 1989.

LAVENIR, C.B. *La Démocratie et Les Médias Au 20e Siecle.* Paris: Armand Collin. 2000.

NACOS, B.L. *Terrorism & the Media.* New York, NY: Columbia University Press. 2000.

NEVEU, E. *Sociologie des Mouvements Sociaux.* 3eme Edit., Paris: Edit.La Découverte & Syros. 2002.

PY, P. *Le Tourisme: Un Phénomene Economique.* Paris: Documentation Française. 1996.

SERVIER, J. *Le Terrorisme.* Paris: Presses Universitaires de France. 1979.

SCRUTON, R. *A Dictionary of Political Thought*. Pan Book. 1983.

TEKELİOĞLU, Z. *Büyük Sağlık Ansiklopedisi.* Genişletilmiş 3. Baski, Ankara, Erkmen Kitabevi. 1991.

TOSKAY, T. *Turizm: Turizm Olayına Genel Yaklaşım*. İstanbul, Der Yay. 1983.

Turizmde Kriz Yönetimi TC Turizm Bak.Tanıtma Gen.Md., Ankara. 2002.

VERGİLİER, T.M. *Kriz Yönetimi*. İstanbul, Alfa Yay. 2004.

WALZER, M. *De La Guerre et Du Tourisme*. Bayard, Paris. 2004.

ARTICLES

AYTEMİZ, S.O.; BOLAT T. vd. (2004/2): Turizm İşletmelerinde Krizler, Etkileri ve Krizden Çıkış:Kriz Yönetimi. *Verimlilik Dergisi*, Ankara, MPM Yay.

BALENCIE, J.M. (Juillet-Août 2004): Les Mille et Un Visage du Terrorisme Contemporain. *Questions Internationales*, No.8.

BEAULIEU,J.; ESSENBERG,B. (2002): Les Repercussions des Evénements du 11 Septembre 2001 Sur Le Secteur du Transport Aérien. www.ılo.org.

BELAU, D. (Mai 2003): New Threats to Employment in the Travel and Tourism Industry. *Magazine Travail*, OIT.

BENKIMOUN, P. (27 Avril 2003): "Victime du SRAS, Le Canada Critique L'OMS," *www.lemonde.fr*

BİR, A.A. (23 Kasım 2003): "Medya Sınıfı Geçti Devlet Kaldı," www.hurriyetim.com.

BOZDEMİR, M. (1981): "Terör(mü) ve Terörizm(mi)?," *A.Ü.Siyasal Bilgiler Fakültesi Yıllığı*, C:VI. Ankara.

CEBECİ,U.(04.05.2003): "Yolcu Uçaklarına Füzesavar," *www. hurriyetim.com.*

CETTINA, N. (2001): "L'Antiterrorisme en Question: de l'Attentat de la Rue Marbeuf Aux Affaires Corses," Michalon, Paris.

COLLIER, E. (07.01.2002): "Des Jeux Oliympiques Sous Tres Haute Surveillance,"   www.lemonde.fr/cgi-bin/ACHATS/ acheter.cgi?offre=ARCHIVES&type_item-ART.

EMSEN,Ö.S.;DEĞER, M.K. (2004): "Turizm Üzerine Terörizmin Etkileri:1984–2001 Türkiye Deneyimi," *Akdeniz Üniversitesi İİBF Dergisi*, No:7.

ERKMEN, S. (Ekim:2001): "11 Eylül 2001: Terörizmin Yeni Miladı," *Stratejik Analiz*, ASAM, Sayı: XVIII.

FEAREY, R.A. (1978): "Introduction to International Terrorism," *International Terrorism in The Contemporary World*, Ed.L.B.Kress&M.G.Wanek.

FLUKIGER, J.M. (11 Mai 2005). "Livre:Le Terrorisme Entre Questions d'Ethique, de Définition et de Responsabilité," www.terrorisme.net/ p/article_155.shtm.

GASSIN, R. (2004): "Conclusions," *Jeune-Ville-Violence*, sous la direction de N. Sillamy, Paris, L'Harmattan.

GOLDRING, M. (2002): "Sortir De La Terreur En Irlande Du Nord," *Penser La Violence*, Paris, IHESI.

GIRVAN, N., (20 Septembre 2001): Tourism, Terrorisme et Commerce. www.acs-aec.org.

GIRVAN, N., (Décembre 2001): Les Compagnies Aériennes Régionales en Crise. *L'Ambassade de France aux Etats Unis.*

HANDSZUH, H.F., (22–23 February 2001): Quality of Tourism Development. *Symposium on Tourism Services*, UNWTO, Geneva/Switzerland.

HERMAN, C. (11 Octobre 2005): Crise Dans Les Organisations. www.wikipedia.org.

JOHNSON, P. (1980): *The Seven Deadly Sins of Terrorism. International Terrorism: Challange and Reponse*, ed. B.N., The Jonathan Institute, Jerusalem.

KAHRAMAN, N. (26 Nisan 2003): Savaştan Sonra Türk Turizmi. *Cumhuriyet Gazetesi.*

KONGAR, E. (22 Ağustos 2005): Beşinci Terör Dalgası: Soğuk Savaş Kalıntısı Örgütler. www.kongar.org.

KORKMAZ, E. (17 Nisan 1998): Laleli Pazarını Kaybetmeyelim. *İTO Gazetesi*, İstanbul.

KAYA, İ. (Ekim: 2004): Uluslararası Terörizmin Yasaklanması Çabaları. *Türk Harb-İş Dergisi*, Sayı: 210, Ankara.

KELLY, J.M.; MİTCHELL, H.T. (1984): Transnational Terrorism and the Western Elite Press. *Media Power in Politics*, Washington, CQ Press.

KEROURIO, P. (09.08.2004): Tourisme et Terrorisme Dans Le Monde. www.geotourweb.com/nouvellepage12.htm.

KÜÇÜKALTAN, D. (2004): Le Tourisme Comme La Cible Des Crises Globals et Le Modele Des Informations Filtrées Au Processus D'Administration De La Crise. *La Gestion Des Crises Et La Gestion Des Risques Dans L'Industrie Du Tourisme: Amforth World Tourism Forum 2004*, Akdeniz Üniversity, Antalya.

LAÇİNER, S. (10.10.2005): Yeni Terörizm Yasası: İngiltere PKK ve DHKPC'yi Yasaklıyor mu? www.turkishweekly.net.

MAFFESOLI, M. (1997): Télévision, Culture et Violence. *Violence et Télévision*, Paris, Presses de la Sorbonne Nouvelle.

MAYER, R.; LAFOREST, M. (1990): Probleme Social:Concept Et Les Principales Ecoles Théoriques. *Revue Service Social*, Vol:39, No:2, Québec.

MİSEREY, Y. (5 Décembre 2001): L'Agriculture, Premier Pollueur De La Seine. *Le Figaro*.

MORGİL, O. (2002): Terörün Sanayi Sektörü Üzerindeki Etkileri. *Dünyada ve Türkiye'de Terör Konferansı Bildirileri*, Ankara, TCMB Yay.

MOWFORTH, M. (Novembre 2003): Tourism, Terrorism and Climate Change. *Workshop on Climate Change and Tourism: Assessment and Coping Strategies*, NATO, Warsaw.

OKUMUŞ, F. (2001): 2001 Yılı Başında Ortaya Çıkan Ekonomik Krizin Bodrum'daki Konaklama İşletmeleri Üzerine Etkileri. *2. Ulusal Türkiye Turizmi Sempozyumu*, İzmir, Dokuz Eylül Üniv.

ÖVET, T. (22.08.2005): Suçluların Geri Verilmesinin Terörle Mücadeledeki Rolü. **www.icisleri.gov.tr/id/dergi/446 189 214.doc**.

PAZARLIOĞLU, V. (2001): 1980–1990 Döneminde Türkiye'de İç Göç Üzerine Ekonometrik Model Çalışması. *5. Ulusal Ekonometri ve İstatistik Sempozyumu*, Çukurova Üniv., Adana.

PHENG, L.S.; HO, D.K.H. (1999): Crisis Management: Survey of Property Development Firms. *Property Management*, Vol: 17–3'den; VERGİLİER, TÜZ, M. (2004): *Kriz Yönetimi*, 3.Bsk., İstanbul, Alfa Yay.

PIZAM, A.; FLEISCHER, A. (2001): Severity vs. Frequency of Acts of Terrorism: Which Has a Larger Impact on Tourism Demand? *The*

Center for Agricultural Economic Research, Working Paper No: 20117, Israel.

POMONTİ, J.C. (5 Avril 2003): L'Asie du Sud-Est est Contrainte de Renoncer A La Manne Du Tourisme. *Le Monde*.

SAYIN, Ü. (24 Temmuz 2005): Biyolojik ve Kimyasal Savaş. **www. biyotek.com.tr/makale/sayı16/biyolojikvekimyasalsavaş.doc**.

SHAPIRO, J.& BENEDICTE, S.(Mars 2003): The French Experience of Counter-terrorism. *Social Science Module, Survival*: 45, 1.

TANRISEVDİ, A. (Temmuz-Eylül 2004): Yönetici Bakışı İle Seyahat Acentalarında Dışsal Kaynaklı Kriz Olgusu. *Seyahat ve Otel İşletmeciliği Dergisi*, Yıl:1, Sayı:1.

TÜRKEŞ, M. (1999): Vulnerability of Turkey to Desertification With Respect to Precipitation and Aridity Conditions. *Journal of Engineering and Environmental Science*, No: 23, TUBİTAK.

TÜRKEŞ, M. (Ekim: 2004): Küresel İklim Değişikliği ve Olası Sonuçları. *Hava Kuvvetleri Dergisi*, Sayı: 348, Ankara.

VARLIER, O. (21 Ağustos 2005): Türk ve Ege Turizminin Geleceği. www.esiad.org.tr/esiad.nsf/0/ 1E95E2B003672912C2256DB2004F062A?OpenDocument.

ZÜLAL, A. (Ekim: 2001): Biyolojik Silahlar. *Bilim ve Teknik,* Sayı: 407.

OTHER PUBLICATIONS

http://arsiv3.hurriyet.com.tr/yazarlar/yazar/0, 10.06.2005.

http://forum.mezun.com/forum/messageview.cfm?catid, 05.03.2004.

www.angelfire.com./folk/sosyolojik, 08.20.2003.

www.antalya.pol.tr/index.php?option=com content, 24.03.2004.

www.aym.itu.edu.tr/terorist/12.pdf+Oklohama+city+sald, 08.22.2005.

www.bilkent.edu.tr/~bilheal/aykonu/Ay2003/may03, 05.03.2003.

www.byegm.gov.tr/YAYINLARIMIZ/DISBASIN/2005/01/
04×01×05htm, 11.21.2003.

www.byegm.gov.tr/YAYINLARIMIZ/DISBASIN/2003/11/
21×11×0.3HTM, 01.04.2005.

www.christusrex.org/wwwl/news/7-96/fm7-23-96.html, 11.04.2005.

www.cnnturk.com/BİLİM_TEKNOLOJİ/haber_detay.asp?, 18.08.2005

www.dtm.gov.tr, 07.28.2002.

www.dtm.gov.tr/ead/DTDERGİ/tem98/kuresel/htm.htm, 12.30.2000.

www.dtm.gov.tr/pazaragiris/ulkeler/urd, 10.02.2005

www.dumlupinar.edu.tr/tr/ssa/biyolojik.htm, 23.01.2005.

www.fr.wikipedia.org/wiki/Crise, 04.06.2005

www.geotourweb.com/nouvellepage12htm, 01.03.2005.

www.havais.org.tr/metinler/brifing_20.doc, 22.03.2006

www.hurriyetim.com.tr/haber/0, 09.13.2005.

www.ilo.org/public/french/dialogues/sector/techmeet/imhcto1/
update.pdf, 20.03.2006.

www.ilo.org/public/french/dialogue/sector/techmeet/imhct01/
update2.pdf, 20.03.2006.

www.ilsole24ore.com, 07.01.2001.

www.kongar.org, 06.02.2005

www.lemonde.fr.web/article

www.linternante.com, 07.24.2005.

www.mediasnews.com/chrono/chrono1993php, 12.11.2004.

www.muhasebat.gov.tr, 08.18.2005

www.ntvmsnbc.com/news/, 01.14.2002.

www.sakarya.pol.tr/sizler/teror.asp, 09.06.2005

www.tbmm.gov.tr/develop/owa/
tbmm_basin_aciklamalari_sd.aciklama?p1=5467, 05.21.2004.

www.terrorisme.net/p/article_166.shtml, 05.11.2005.

www.turizimdebusabah.com/devam_popup.asp, 04.13.2003.

www.un.org/apps/newsFr/storyF.
asp?NewsID=1007000Cr=Terorisme&Cr1=Annan, 03.10.2005.

www.wikipedia.org/wiki/Crise, 04.12.2006

www.world-tourism.org/francais/newsroom/Releases, 03.08.2002.

www.world-tourism.org/francais/newsroom/Releases/more_releases/
Juin2002/chiffres2001.htm, 03.03.2005

www.world-tourism.org/market_research/facts/highlights, 08.03.2005.

www.yesil.org./teror/irapkk.htm, 10.20.2005.

978-0-595-38998-8
0-595-38998-8